Eighteen Holes in My Head

Milton Gross

EIGHTEEN HOLES

McGRAW-HILL BOOK COMPANY, INC.

New York

Toronto

London

IN MY HEAD

Foreword by JIMMY DEMARET

Illustrations by JOHN PIEROTTI

EIGHTEEN HOLES IN MY HEAD

Library of Congress Catalog Card Number: 59-14449

SECOND PRINTING
24972

To all of us
Who have ballmarks on our clubs
Where they shouldn't be,
Scars on our souls
Only we can see
And chains on our wrists
We can't get free.

CONTENTS

o o o o o o o o o

FOREWORD

○ ○ ○ ○ ○ ○ ○ ○ ○ ○

From the moment I put a golf club into Milton Gross'
hands for the first time I was sure that nothing good could
come of it—until he put the hilarious pages of *Eighteen
Holes in My Head* into *my* hands.

Milt often has threatened to put a dent in my skull with
a club, but he's never appreciated how tempted I have been
to put one in his when I've heard him tell people I was his
first instructor. But after suffering through his shame, embarrassment and pain in these pages, I promise I'll never
mistake his skull for the ball. He has been sufficiently pun-
ished. By becoming a chronicler of the misery of the game
I love, he has made everything up to me—as well as to so
many of his brothers in anguish who love it as much as I do.

This is a funny book because it's about people in a
funny game who still can laugh through their tears. That
makes it human. I don't want to sound too highbrow here,
because I'm not and never have been a highbrow guy. I just
like people, and having had a God-given opportunity to be
able to play golf fairly well, I've gotten around to most
places in the world where it is played. I've had the chance
to meet all kinds of people playing golf. They're the nicest
people, and they're never nicer than when they're laughing
at their own misery.

That's the best kind of humor—being able to make fun of yourself—and that's what Milt has done here. Milt is Everyman. Not just the hacker hoping to break 100, but the pro and low-handicap amateur who suffer as much by making one or two poor shots during a round as Milt has suffered by making so many.

He says he's never going to play a round with me again, but I'm sure he'll change his mind. I enjoy playing with him, just as I enjoy playing with other friends who experience a little trouble on the golf course. Once I dubbed a shot while playing with Milt and he looked at me with real astonishment on his face and said:

"You, too, Jimmy?"

"Yes, Milt," I said, "me, too."

I guess that's just what Milt's done in *Eighteen Holes in My Head*.

You can read it and say to yourself, "Him, too, the poor slob." Him and you and you and you and me, but what a wonderful way to suffer.

Jimmy Demaret

Eighteen Holes in My Head

ONE

○ ○ ○ ○ ○ ○ ○ ○ ○ ○

The girl I left behind me

JIMMY DEMARET stepped to the tee with practiced and professional ease. He swung, and the little white ball became a diminishing dot in the distance. It landed on the fairway, hopped like a scared rabbit and ended its roll just a few feet from the green.

"That's all there is to it," said the three-time winner of the Masters Tournament, who once was known as golf's happy jester. "Now you try it."

Those were the last words I heard before I died. Perhaps it would be more accurate to say I'm still living, but it is just a living death. It was six years ago that I took a golf club in my hands for the first time, and I live for the day when I will be able to part Demaret's hair with a 2-iron, because, thanks to him, I dwell in a community of grief, helplessly marooned in the sea of hope that is the purgatory of dufferdom.

It is not really true that golf is a game which was invented by the Scots. It was conceived by a sadist to be practiced by masochists. Actually, no matter how you slice it, it is not a game. It is a narcotic. Once the bug bites it is fatal. You don't *play* golf, you *fight* it.

1

Some addicts say it's not really the game which is crazy, just the golfer, but there must be something essentially wrong with a game in which a left-hander such as myself, who has spent nearly half a century using a south paw eating, writing, gesticulating and whacking the kids after a normal day on what laughingly is known as the links, must concentrate on the right arm for power.

Do you want the ball to go up, then hit down. Do you want it to go right, then swing left. You look in one direction to direct the ball in another. You stand at right angles to your directed line of flight. You take two strokes to go 400 yards and four more to go 4 feet. When you get to where you're going, there's a hole in the ground $4\frac{1}{4}$ inches wide. The rest of the world is all around it, but you're expected to deposit the ball into the hole.

Maybe it would be best if all would-be golfers deposited themselves in the hole. (It could be done, of course, as it is well known that every golfer's head comes to a point in a relatively short period of time.) Instead, they go to pros, hoping to improve their game. They'd be better off going to psychoanalysts. Who would you rather have peering into the eighteen holes in your head?

There is a solution, of course. You could take the clubs out to the back yard and become a model husband by helping the wife to beat the carpets. Or you could cut off their heads and convert them into pool sticks.

Me? I've tried both, but neither has worked. As with cigarettes, I've quit the game regularly, but have come back just as regularly in the hope that once, just once, I'll be able to place the drives, fairway woods, pitches, chips and putts together. At night I lie awake picturing the perfect swing, but in the daytime it evades me as the wispy smoke of the reverie fades into reality. I'm "over-proed," overwhelmed and over par. I have a friend whose wife solemnly swears that her husband keeps a 7-iron at his bedside at night. The poor woman slept with one eye open for weeks, fearful

that poppa planned to bash in her skull. But lately she's resting easily. All that's been cut up has been the carpet on which the old man has taken to practicing chip shots during the night.

My wife has only herself to blame. Originally she encouraged me to join the ranks of souls in limbo. Then, after I'd become an addict of sticks and tees, going to great lengths to use them, she suggested none too subtly that I take my clubs and get lost permanently.

There was, for instance, the week-end I weaseled away for three days of hell at Shawnee-on-the-Delaware, Pennsylvania, the golfing resort run by Fred Waring, who soothes you with his music, confuses you on his tricky course, and addles you completely with the mixer he invented.

In any event, I was 100 miles from home when I suddenly realized that I'd packed a bag but left it behind. I made a screeching U turn, hurtled through lights and up one-way streets going the wrong way and arrived at the house in time to catch the missus still in her self-pitying I-am-a-deserted-wife role.

"What's the matter, Enoch Arden?" she said, biting off the words as though they were hard candy. "Did you forget something?"

"I forgot my clothes," I said, sounding as though it were not unusual for a man to go off for a week-end and leave a bag behind (nothing personal, dear).

"I know darned well it wasn't your golf clubs that you forgot," she said.

It isn't, of course, that the wife minds so much being deserted. It's just that she doesn't like being marooned in a suburban town when the only car in the family is off cooking under a broiling sun on a golf-course parking lot, while she is cooking at home, but not over the stove.

To solve the problem I once tried to go into hock to buy a second car, but the missus would have none of it. "Look

4

how convenient it will be," I pleaded. "You can shop, go to the P.T.A., never have to worry about the car pool for the kids. You'll have a car of your own. I'll have mine. There'll be no more arguments."

That started the biggest argument of all. "Don't think I'm going to provide the salve for your guilty conscience," she argued. "You're not buying the car to make it easier for me. You want to buy it so that you can swing those sticks every week-end with an easy mind. If you want to play that silly game, then be a man and take your punishment when you get home."

It's an even bet I can stand her off in any normal domestic squabble, but when she makes my golf an issue at home no less torturous than it is on the course, what chance for happiness has a guy who has been sneered at by the caddy, who has ventured into parts of the course the architect never knew existed, suffered the indignity of having a couple of *women* ask if they could play through, and missed by one stroke breaking 100 by four-putting the eighteenth?

As I've learned through bitter experience, golf is a diabolical contrivance, but it is not so devilish as the woman scorned for a driving range. Accordingly, I underwent a truly scary experience recently when my spouse unreasonably began to be reasonable about my misspent hours on country real estate. One night we had a date to go out to dinner, and you could have knocked me over with a goosenecked putter when she suggested I spend the day playing golf and she would meet me at the club.

She was on time, but I tarried awhile at the nineteenth hole, reliving the horrible afternoon. Nevertheless, she was all charm and loveliness when I met her.

"Well," she asked, as though she really cared, "how did you hit them?"

That's when I knew. That's when the great awakening light came, with the full force of the golf ball that caromed off my skull on the fourteenth green of the first full eighteen holes I'd ever struggled through. She was trying to get me to hate myself, hoping that I would transfer that emotion to golf and would quit the silly game entirely. She wanted me to think how easy it was for others, but how hard it was for me.

"How did I hit them?" A fine question. How do I always hit them? I'm so full of theory and so empty of fulfillment that I carry a golf ball around with me constantly, in my throat. I'm loose and full of ginger until I get to the tee, and then if you whacked my arms they would splinter like icicles. I am a long-ball hitter, but the woods are full of long hitters like me. The next caddy up pales and quails when he sees my bag being carried out. I have kept Spalding's in business turning out balls for me to maim. The fortitude of at least two dozen pros has worn thin before my ineptitude.

Once I played a new course with the Long Island pro, Jack Oliver. Jack figured he was working on me while all the time I was inadvertently working on him. He would never admit that his patience would run out sooner than my unproductive energy. He kept coming up with gimmicks designed to straighten out my slice, but I would start to hook. He'd get the hook straightened away, but the irons would start to melt.

Oliver valiantly stayed with me as I struggled through the round. I asked him what the caddy should be paid for the eighteen.

"Be good to him," Jack said. "He's had a hard day with you."

"I will," I said, "but what's the fee here? What shall I give him?"

"Why," said Jack, moving rapidly toward the clubhouse, "don't you give him your clubs?"

On one occasion Oliver called me at home. He said he and Moe Leff, the Joe Palooka artist, were planning a book on golf instruction. He invited me to write the captions for

6

Leff's illustrations. I suggested this was like getting the class dunce to swap places with teacher.

"Why me, of all people?" I said.

"You, of all people," Oliver said, "because nobody I know has had more trouble on a golf course. Only those who are having trouble need an instruction book. The others don't read, they play. You can bring the writing down to the lowest common denominator. Any problems anybody else has, you've had."

Golf has been called many things, few of which could be uttered over a nationwide television hookup. An exception was former Israeli ambassador Abba Eban's description of the game. Ed Murrow was interviewing Mr. Eban on Person-to-Person when Mr. Eban described his delight at golf's perversity.

"Playing the game," he said, "I have learned the meaning of humility. It has given me an understanding of the futility of human effort."

Now Mr. Eban can speak nine languages, and if you examine his words as carefully as some of us examine the ball while lining up a putt or standing at address before taking a shot, you'll see that what he said would be perfectly apt in any of them.

There are golfers, this one included, who become unnerved and embarrassed to be reminded that the ball, unlike an egg, will not hatch no matter how long it is stood over. There are others, of course, who so lack confidence that occasionally they'll stay over the ball long enough to make it appear as though they're praying over it. Partners in a foursome sometimes take a dim view of such religious observance. One day a golfer in my group, casting his eyes in my direction, suggested, "I've seen people pray in a lot of places, but never on the first tee."

"Mister," said the caddy, "it's not the prayer that's bothering me. It's the time that man's taking waiting for the answer."

The only other time I'd heard it suggested that golf might provide a spiritual experience was a late afternoon when I'd taken an iron and a practice ball into the back yard to warm up a bit.

Unknown to me, the wife was spying through the kitchen window. After flubbing a few shots, I looked all about me to see if the neighbors were watching. No one was visible —and then I saw my loyal helpmate with a look akin to outrage on her face.

"I thought you'd decided to give up that silly game," she said.

"I'd move heaven and earth to be able to play it respectably," I answered, clearly ducking a direct reply to her remark.

With maddening deliberation, she examined the back yard, which had been chewed to bits with the effectiveness of a roto-tilling machine. "From the looks of that lawn," she finally said, "I guess all you really have left to move is heaven."

Since Mr. Eban has stressed the seldom discussed spiritual values of this humbling game which has been foisted upon civilization as a form of healthy relaxation, I am certain fellow sufferers will not mind my dwelling for a moment on my own adventures into humility and futility in this "sodforsaken" sport. These are refined experiences—gathered while undergoing the most refined kind of torture since the invention of the Chinese water treatment.

There was, for instance, the time I idiotically agreed to play a round with Jimmy Demaret and Vic Ghezzi.

They had qualified for the National Open and were practicing at the Concord International in Kiamesha Lake, New York, before leaving for Toledo, where it was to be played.

"Vic and I are playing a round," Demaret said. "You be the third and we'll get a fourth."

"Good," said Ray Parker, the Concord's general manager,

who was present the day Demaret gave me my first lesson. "Let's see how expert you've become."

It seemed like a fine idea to me. Here I was getting the opportunity to play with two of the world's finest teachers and shotmakers just before golf's biggest tournament. It was exciting, only the exhilaration turned to emotion, the emotion to concern, the concern to fear, and the fear into hives when a gallery began to collect for a clinic which was to be conducted by Demaret and Ghezzi before we went out for our match. At the conclusion of the clinic Jimmy invited the gallery to follow us around the course to witness how shots are made. It was to be a practical demonstration of his teaching. Suddenly it dawned on me that I was about to be cast in the role of guinea pig.

"We'll go out in a few minutes," Demaret said as I started to congeal in the hot summer heat. "I just want to call Toots. I'll say hello for you."

Toots is Toots Shor, the New York restaurant owner who is a bosom buddy to most sporting celebrities. His bosom has slipped so extensively, though, that now when he goes out on the golf course he is a self-confessed "victim of circumference." He describes his ailment this way: "When I stand close enough to the ball to reach it, I can't see it. When I see it, I can't reach it."

I have an analogous problem. I stand too close to the ball when I hit it, too. And sometimes I'm standing too close to it *after* I've hit it.

"Don't say hello to Toots for me," I said. "I think you'd better say good-bye. I don't think I will make it to the first tee."

I'd covered enough pro tournaments as a sports columnist to have an accurate image of the crowds surrounding the tees and lining the fairways. My wrists began to itch. Large welts appeared on them and the itch spread over my body. Parker introduced me to a man named Maury Wallace, who was to be the fourth. He looked composed.

10

"This will be the climax of my life, playing with Demaret," Wallace said.

There must have been 500 spectators waiting to follow our great foursome. "There must be an easier way to die," I muttered.

"You and I will cut up Ghezzi and Wallace," Demaret said. I wiped my forehead. It was only cold sweat. I felt as though I had already been slashed.

Ever the gallant, Demaret bent, teed up a snow-white ball, patted my shoulder and said, "Show me the way, partner."

"Remember what we've been talking about," Ghezzi said. "Remember about finishing the shot the way Ted Williams hits a baseball. Come all the way through with your hands at impact. Rotate your wrists into the follow-through and watch that ball fly."

Ghezzi was talking about finishing the shot. At that moment I was concerned only over my inability to start it. I froze as I addressed the ball. My body simply refused to turn to get the club away from the ball in the backswing. I stepped away. This time I didn't pray. I was shaking too hard. There was a tremor in my neck that wouldn't stop. I kept thinking perhaps I could suggest that I would set them up for the entire gallery if they would just go back to the bar.

Eventually I had to swing. The ball went bloop-bloop-bloop just about that far down the fairway. Somebody in the crowd snickered. If I hadn't wanted to kill myself more, I would probably have tried to kill him. My recollection of the round is hazy, as though I had been caught in a burning building through which firemen were spraying gallons of water. I do have three clear recollections, however. On the second hole a spectator sidled up and said: "I'd give anything to be in your place."

"And I'd give anything to be in *yours,*" I said, and I meant it.

11

On the third hole another spectator asked for my autograph, with a wise grin. "Whenever I play a bad round," he said, "I'll look at your signature and know there's somebody who once felt worse than I do."

In the clubhouse after the funeral, Phil Greenwald, who books the Concord's acts and deals with such performers as Buddy Hackett, Alan King, Jackie Miles and other laugh producers, asked how I could have been foolish enough to go out and play with the pros.

"They," I said, "supply the golf. I supply the comedy relief."

TWO

○ ○ ○ ○ ○ ○ ○ ○ ○

Dr. Livingstone, I presume

ONLY SLIGHTLY ashamed, but utterly confused, I confess that I have played rounds where the other three players in the foursome became total strangers to me in the long distances between tee and green. When I finally hack my way out of the underbrush, I am never surprised if one of them extends a hand and says, "Dr. Livingstone, I presume."

Once at Grossinger's Country Club in Grossinger, New York, I had a caddy who knew me from a previous, bitter, body-rending experience. At the first tee he asked if I'd lend him a dime to make a phone call. When he returned to the tee, he hefted my bag with the resigned shrug of a man going into a battle from which he doubted he'd return. I asked what had been so important to require a phone call after the starter had summoned us to the tee.

"I wanted to call the wife to tell her not to wait dinner," he said wistfully, "and to kiss the kids goodnight for me."

Obviously he was a comedian. Otherwise why did he drop to his knees and kiss the grass when, through some miracle, a shot of mine caromed off a tree, bounced off a rock and landed out of the rough?

It was also at Grossinger's that I had another caddy, this one named Irish, who had a sense of humor to match his name and who profoundly told me I had broken the course record when I sliced a ball across two fairways and into an apple orchard out of bounds.

The ball was brand new. Irish started across the fairway to see if he could retrieve it. It was mid-afternoon and we had been out since just after breakfast without a lunch break. Perhaps Irish wanted to fill his protesting stomach with apples. Even if they were sour, they might improve the wry look on his face.

"Come back here," I called to his retreating form. "A guy hits a ball that badly doesn't deserve to get it back."

"A guy hits a ball that badly," Irish said, "deserves it as a remembrance."

My whole purpose in rehashing this tragic personal history in what jocularly is known as a sport is to forewarn the newcomer what wonderfully horrible things lie ahead. The inveterate duffer doesn't need the warning. He knows that if he had four arms he would probably be twice as bad as he is with two. With a normal complement, he tries twice as hard, maybe, but gets only half as confused. The real confusion, however, doesn't come until years later, when he realizes that what looked like the simplest game in the world is possibly the most difficult.

Paradoxically, I felt my keenest sense of appreciation and deepest feeling of despair at the Pasadena Country Club in St. Petersburg, Florida, where elderly folks on the golf course are a common sight. Late one afternoon I was tallying my card when an octogenarian came off the eighteenth, fairly skipping in delight and in a quavering voice declared, "By keeriminy, I think I'm beginning to get the hang of this game."

Knowing that I hadn't even begun to get the hang of it, I sought to learn the old man's secret. "Sir," I said, "I admired the way you played your approach to the last green."

"Pretty nifty, wasn't it, young fella?" he said.

"Would you mind telling me how old you are?" I asked.

"Eighty-four my next birthday," he said, pleased.

"And how long have you been playing golf?"

He made a mental calculation. "Over sixty years," he said, "and I think I finally got it."

I moved away stunned. Sixty years and he only thought he had it. Roughly, that would make me a hundred and something before I'd get it, and I doubted I'd hold on that long. But what could I do? I was hooked as surely as though I'd gone for hasheesh.

For all practical purposes every golfer is an addict egging somebody else on to the vice. Over the entrance to every golf club there should be a sign reading, "Abandon hope, all ye who enter here." In fact, I was told that the day I started, but who listened? More accurately, who heard? There was a ringing in my ears that I mistook for the song of the eagles and birdies. A bird can't fly on one wing, however, and a golfer can't play on one lesson. I had to go back for more.

The whole thing really started as a gag. I was at the Concord Hotel and didn't want to drive back to New York on traffic-heavy Route 17 on a Sunday. But I had a deadline to meet for my column in the *New York Post,* and I cast about me for ideas. I recalled the admonition my editor, Ike Gellis once gave me: "You think golf is a silly game," he had said, "because you never played it. *Try* it and see, but do it right. Get a pro to instruct you."

I phoned Jimmy Demaret, the Concord pro, to arrange for instructions. "I never held a club in my hand before," I told him. "Would you show me what this game is all about, and I'll write tomorrow's column on what I've learned." Little did I appreciate then that I must have sounded like the new female member at Green Acres Country Club in Glencoe, Illinois, who brought a visiting lady friend to the practice tee. "You taught me how to play

15

yesterday," she said to her pro instructor. "Today I want you to teach my friend."

"Why just me?" Demaret said. "I've got six other pros here. Let's make it a good lesson. We'll each instruct you in one element of the game."

When I got to the course, Demaret and his assistants were waiting for me. I opened the proceedings. "What," I asked my instructors, "is the primary point of instruction?"

"Your grip," said Demaret, who bent to arrange my hand on the club.

"Now," said Lou Nash, "keeping your stance at right angle with your imaginary line of flight is very important."

"You don't want to be too anxious," said Stu Boyle. "The average player hits at the ball from the top of the swing. He just won't wait until he reaches the hitting area before applying his hand and arm action. He sees that ball sitting there looking so easy to hit and he can't wait to do it. He tries to get at it before he gets to the bottom of his swing and then all he has left is a push."

Behind me I felt other pushing. Pete Lipchik was shifting my feet. Jimmy Basile was trying to get me to bend at the waist without slumping my shoulders. "You're sort of a short man," Lipchik said. "Your center of gravity must be closer to the ground."

"My what?" I said.

"Your butt," said Demaret. "You'll never hit the ball standing the way you are. If you're going to hit it right you'll have to sit on the ball. All good golfers sit down on it before they hit it."

"Bring the club back now," said Ansel Snow.

"Wait a minute now," said Basile, "That grip isn't right. The inverted V of your thumb and forefinger isn't pointing to the left side of your face."

"Look down your shaft," said Demaret, "if you can see only two or three knuckles of your hands you're gripping

16

right. If you see four you're over too far. If you see only one you're under too far."

"Right now," I said, "I would like to look down at that tee and see the head of the guy who suggested all this. I'd swing this club and I wouldn't miss."

"Suppose you swing it then," said Demaret, "and think of the guy. Pretend that little white ball has black hair on it, but don't try to kill it. Just mash it a little."

"Okay," I replied, "but there is one thing wrong. The face of this club is on the wrong side."

"I don't get it," said Demaret. The six other pros reflected his confusion.

"I guess I failed to mention," I said, "that I'm left-handed and this is a right-handed club."

"Your first lesson," said Demaret, "is over. Ben Hogan can rest easy."

As Demaret and I walked to the clubhouse, he said, "Try to remember the important points we've been telling you. When you address the ball, these are your check points: Is your grip correct? Is your stance correct? Are your toes turned out? Remember to coordinate your hands, your pivot and your clubhead. Are you relaxed?"

As I think back on it that last question was the tiny fissure which has led to my cracking up. The most advanced medical brains in the universe have yet to discover a way for a man to relax himself, and looking at a golf ball is not the cure. Golf may produce pep and vim, but inevitably rigor mortis sets in.

The fact is, many a pro has told me that the old adage "Physician, heal thyself" is one of the jokes certain to stimulate a belly laugh around a golf club. There is one pro, in fact, who became seriously ill on the night before a pro-member tournament. He called in a member, who was also a doctor, to treat him.

"I'll take care of you," the doctor said, "but only if you tell me the secret."

"The secret of what?" croaked the pro, his brow burning with fever.

"The secret," the doctor repeated, his own eyes burning with a heat which can only come from years of frustration on the course. "I mean *the secret*. You pros know it, but you never reveal it. You're all together against us. What's the one thing that makes a golfer a golfer."

"Doc," the pro pleaded, wondering if he'd picked on a madman and apprehensive because all golfers are slightly mad, "I'm burning up. Do something for me. There's no secret. I can't tell you a thing."

"In that case," said the doctor, "swallow a couple of aspirin. That's about as much advice as you've given me all these years."

As I drove home the following morning Demaret's instructions kept whirling through my mind, and I determined to see if I had absorbed anything.

After dinner I visited a driving range near my home. After spraying two pails of balls in all directions and exhausting myself, my first feelings of inferiority began to set in. This couldn't be, I told myself. It should be relatively simple to hit the ball hard enough and straight enough to make at least some progress toward that little flag flapping impudently over the green. I had seen it done by little boys, fat women and men with thick glasses. Why not me?

It is a singular characteristic of most men who may have been partially proficient in sports in their younger days that they do not learn how unathletic they are until they try golf. A fine gentleman named A. B. Bindursky of Lepanto, Arkansas, who would drive 50 miles for a game on a cow pasture, once told me that a man begins chasing a golf ball when he no longer can chase anything else. My own feeling is that it would be simpler, less expensive and far less wearing on body and mind to chase just about anything else.

Scarcely aware of what I was doing, I signed up for a course of lessons with Jack Mackie, whose family once was on spitting terms with every wind which blows over Carnoustie—the famous and maddening course in Scotland. For the first two lessons, however, I wondered if Mackie's name really wasn't Arthur Murray. The guy never put a ball on the tee or let me try to put club to ball. Instead he sang to me tuneful snatches of the Skater's Waltz, while I was shown how to swing my hips to and fro in rhythm.

"Learn that," he said, "and you've learned the basic elements of the swing."

"Learn that," I said, "and I might win a prize in a rhumba contest. I want to be like Hogan, not Hernando."

"Never mind the wisecracks," Mackie answered. "All you newcomers are the same," and he began again to croon ... "One ... two ... one ... two. ..."

After seven lessons Mackie had me driving, pitching and chipping, but always with a prop. One day he placed a chair at my right hip as I addressed the ball. The idea was that my hip had to hit the chair top just at the start of the downswing. The forward motion of the hip, he said, brought the arms, the club and the clubhead around properly to hit the ball. Another day he placed a pebble on the mat 3 inches in front of the tee and said if the pebble were hit it would mean that the ball had been hit with the proper follow-through. A third time he had me grasp the clubhead and swing at a tee with the handle to feel that proper motion of a finished shot.

Finally I decided I was ready to try golf for real. Mackie didn't agree, but he knew he couldn't dissuade me. He tried another tack.

"Anybody goes out in this heat," he said, "has got to be crazy."

"I," I said, "will make you proud of me."

"Let's not get personal," he said.

So there I was on the fifteenth hole at Wheatley Hills Golf Club on Long Island, where the late Willie Klein, the club pro, had no idea how much of a backward step the royal and ancient game was about to take.

One of my threesome was Lou Effrat, the gentleman horseplayer who writes sports for *The New York Times* and is affectionately known as "Tap-out Louie." True to his name, Lou tapped out after the first nine—holes, not races. It proved that a *Times* man has sense, even if he can't play golf. It wasn't any more than 110 degrees in the shade. However, it wasn't the heat that chased Effrat so much as the energy he expended trying to help me find the two balls (at a buck and a quarter a throw) I lost on my first three swings on the first hole.

I thought nothing worse could happen. It was only a game. I remembered what Demaret said, and for a few wonderful moments I relaxed and it helped. Into each rough some balls must fall, but a few of my shots landed on the fairway. Some of the pitches and chips managed to avoid the traps. On the fourteenth I actually produced a par.

Then came the song of birdies and eagles. "Always keep your head down," I had been told. I was doing just that in a deep trap to the left of the green, which must be a sand brother to the Grand Canyon, and was unaware that my remaining companion, Ray Lavenger, a gin-rummy partner of Tap-out Louie, was doing the same in the trap to the right. Lavenger blasted his best shot of the day. It arched beautifully as the wedge bit under the ball. Only it was a little too strong. Instead of hitting the green, the ball overshot and hit me on the head. I haven't gotten over it yet.

There is no obvious aftermath from a whack on the skull, although I'm told the effect is often latent and likely permanent. It is something like an inoculation, and nobody knows what strange antibodies swing into action once the venom has worked its way through your system.

With or without a hit on the head, the golfer is likely to develop some discernible idiosyncrasies. One is a com-

21

pulsive urge to talk to himself. Mumbling and gesticulating, he replays every fluffed shot a hundred times. I have caught myself in a one-man conversation walking down Wilshire Boulevard. "Idiot, can't you remember a thing! You told yourself to pause at the top of your *backswing*. ... You told yourself to hit *through* the ball, not *at* it. ... Hands, hands, use your hands. ... Keep your stupid head down. ... Won't you ever learn? ... What am I doing wrong?"

Another noticeable oddity is a growing predilection for weird golf stories. Sam Levenson, mama's favorite monologist, who says every time he has an urge to play golf he lies down until the urge passes, tells about this golfer friend of his who was playing at Dyker Heights in Brooklyn. Dyker is a public course—in fact it's the wildest and most public course in the world, flying clubs and balls, bags and bagels all over the place. Anything, but anything, can happen at Dyker.

Anyway, this particular day a stranger came up to Levenson's friend and asked if he could play through. Having received permission, the stranger placed a tee in the ground, neglected to place a ball upon it, took a healthy swing at nothing, peered into the distance down the fairway, and smiled in self-satisfied fashion.

"Nice drive, huh?" he said.

"Wait a minute, now," Sam's friend said. "What kind of nonsense is that? You just swung. You didn't hit a ball."

"What difference?" the strange one said. "This way every shot's down the middle and I don't aggravate myself. I'm out in the open air, I'm getting the exercise and have none of the problems. I used to play with a ball. This way's got it beat."

"Come to think of it, that's not a bad idea. Do you mind if I try it with you?"

"Help yourself," the stranger said, "so long as you supply your own tees; and no winter rules."

They went along that way for several holes, both content, both declaring their scores relatively honestly, when Sam's friend suddenly became anguished.

"What did you say you shot on the last hole?" he asked the stranger.

"A four," the man said.

"What about the fairway shot?" he was asked. "You missed that shot completely."

"That was no whiffie," the stranger said, indignantly. "That was a practice swing."

"I don't care what you call it," Sam's friend growled, "but I distinctly heard you grunt when you swung."

With that he set upon the stranger and if it weren't for a couple of caddies in the woods, no doubt still there from the last time they looped for me, the murderer would have gone unapprehended.

Tried by the court, found guilty and sentenced to hang, he was asked by the warden if he had any last request.

"Would it be all right," he asked, "if I take a few practice swings first?"

Another well-known homicide on the links happened when a player took a full backswing, laid open his partner's skull and returned to the clubhouse shouting he had killed the poor soul.

A club member gazed up with an anguished look from a scorecard he was considering not turning in to the handicap committee and asked, "That so? Which club were you swinging?"

"The two iron," moaned the killer.

"It figures," the other said. "That's the same damned club that always gets me into trouble."

THREE

o o o o o o o o o

You can't take it with you

OUTSIDE, the thermometer was threatening to blow its cork and inside the missus thought I had already blown mine. She lifted her head from the pillow in our nicely air-conditioned bedroom just in time to see me packing a bag.

This is always a crucial moment in our home. There she is, looking lovely, her head wrapped in rollers and toilet tissue, all covered by a hair net, and there I am trying to sneak out without explaining where I'm going before breakfast.

"Where," she asked, "are you going in this weather?"

Clearly, it was necessary to be firm and brazen it out. "I'm going to the golf course," I said.

"It's taken me a lifetime," she answered, "to learn that I'm married to a man who has no head on his shoulders."

This of course, is incorrect. My head is not only prominent, but is unsullied by lacquer, toilet tissue and beauty rinse. If I still have a few black strands among the silver, it's only because not every iron is a shank and some of my putts occasionally drop into the cup with a harmonious clank.

To hit a golf ball properly you must do perhaps one hundred things right, but all you have to do to hit it improperly is one thing wrong. And by far the worst thing to do is to stand over the ball, club in hand, puzzling over these pitfalls. As a friend once said to me, "The longer you wait over the ball, the smaller it starts to get, and it's no basketball to begin with."

Harry Obitz, the pro at the Shawnee Country Club, once told me I was truly a unique golfer. "You make twenty mistakes going into your backswing and correct ten of them coming forward, but unfortunately you haven't quite balanced your budget," he said.

Obitz's course is situated on a rise near the Delaware Water Gap, and a few years ago during a torrential rainstorm the entire valley was flooded. The only relatively dry spot in the inundated area was the golf course, and a doe obeying its instincts for self-preservation sought refuge. She found a home on the course, and grew big and strong grazing on the fairways.

One day during this period I had an 8 A.M. tee-off date there with Jackie Gleason of television fame. Gleason showed up with a bag which carried twelve woods, all neatly wrapped in mink club covers. The only two irons in the bag were the wedge and putter, and Jackie wore not one glove, but two.

Maybe that's why the doe took to us. She didn't know a blessed thing about golf, but she recognized class. I stepped to the tee, said my customary benediction over the ball, and waited to hear if there'd be any reply from above. I looked up from the ball to line up my target and there were two beautiful liquid-brown eyes staring into mine. As if that weren't enough, the doe not only was licking her chops, but tried to lick mine as well.

Now we all know you have to get off the first tee to start a round of golf. Under the best of conditions, this is usually a problem for me, and the doe wasn't making it any easier.

26

What was I to do with a doe gazing soulfully into my eyes? It wasn't a case of love at first sight on my part, I can tell you that. If I had had a hunting license, Fred Waring's clientele might well have had venison for dinner that night.

"Shoo!" I shouted ineffectually. "Get out of here!"

The doe didn't budge.

"I don't blame her," Gleason chuckled. "Obviously she has seen you tee off before and knows that the safest place to be when you play is right down the middle."

I became impatient and began poking at the doe with my club. She stood her ground. Then I began swinging at her, but she ducked gracefully. In desperation I lifted her by her front legs and tried to lead her in another direction. I reeled under her weight and the doe and I two-stepped around the tee.

At this point, a red-faced Obitz ran up on the tee. "What's going on here?" he roared. "If you want to waltz with a deer, Gross, do it at the next S.P.C.A. ball."

I retreated to the clubhouse, done in by a doe.

Golf isn't a game, it's a sentence, and the most depressing part of the servitude is that it's self-imposed. Sometimes I catch myself measuring my years on the links as a convict laboriously scratches out his served time on a prison wall. Golf is supposed to be relaxing, but for every day of exhilaration, there's one of depression. And what is a depression, after all, except a hole? And what is a hole? It's the final resting place—if you ever get there—of the golf ball. My final resting place—if I can find an agreeable caddy to bury me—will be a sand trap.

Perhaps it would be best if a caddy simply buries my scorecards, inasmuch as I don't use them any more anyway. Not that I cheat. I merely keep my score in my head and some days my head is more shrunken than others. When some wise guy in the clubhouse inquires what I "played in,"

I answer, "Shirt and pants." Or I'll mutter ambiguously, "Approximately 90." In the varying longitudes in which I play I do not consider it at all amiss to take a little latitude. After all, if the universal golfing complaint is, "I'm hitting the ball well, but I'm just not scoring," why not simply improve my scoring?

The proper attitude would seem to be the one adopted by the two middle-aged pinochle players who had come up in the world. While their wives were taking cha-cha lessons, they discovered golf.

They joined a country club, disdained the pro, and enjoyed the game immensely. At the end of their first round one had shot 220, the other 223.

The 220 player said to his friend, "This is a good game, this golf, but there's not enough action. Let's make it more interesting. Let's play a dollar a hundred."

I have not yet turned to gambling, although sometimes I think Russian roulette would cause me less apprehension than approaching the first tee. Why this should be has never been explained to me satisfactorily. A dozen pros have tried to cure my first-tee jitters.

"Stop worrying," they advise me. "You drive for the show and putt for the dough." This advice has served to create still another problem for me, because of the dough I've lost and the show I've made of myself.

In my case at least, a pro is a better drinking partner than a consultant on why I freeze over a ball and where the rhythm and consistency of my practice swing goes once a real game begins.

Put me on a rubber mat on a practice tee on a driving range and any pro would be proud to display me as a prize pupil. But no sooner do my feet feel grass and I know there's a scorecard in my pocket that needs filling in, than that paradoxical reaction takes place.

My hands begin to sweat and my body itches. All the wonderful instruction I thought I'd absorbed oozes out of my open pores and is replaced by shuddering memories of every bad shot which ever skidded off my clubs. Indecision seizes me and makes me captive. I don't know if I intend to forward press or not. I try to recall whether the clubhead starts back first, or is it the knee, hip or shoulder. I can't make up my mind between a short backswing and a real wind up. Fearful of a slice, I'll employ a hook grip and then wonder whether my feet are positioned correctly.

Once Pat Tiso, the pro at Pine Hollow Country Club in East Norwich, Long Island, tried to cure me by taking the club out of my hand and handing me a pencil and piece of paper.

"I make a living writing," I said smugly.

"All right, bright boy," Pat said, "let's see how many things you can think of at once when you're writing. Just write the word Washington on that paper, but while you're doing it I want you to be spelling Philadelphia mentally."

I looked at him intently, wondering how the pencil would look sticking out of his chest.

"It can't be done," he concluded correctly, "and the ball can't be hit properly if you engage in memory exercises, muscular contortion, or emotional upheaval while you're standing over it."

The pros say, "have one thought in mind, just one," but unless they're better brainwashers than Mao Tse-tung's boys, sure enough that burrowing worm of recollection is bound to rear its ugly head, if you don't lift your own and ... wham. ... "Did anybody see where that one went?" ... "It's right there at your feet, brother." ... "Heh, heh. So it is."

Dr. Cary Middlecoff once suggested to me, at the lush Diplomat Hotel in Hollywood, Florida, that the way to beat indecision was to walk up to the ball, count four and complete your swing at the last count.

"If you wait longer you'll get tensed up," said Middlecoff, who became a pro when he rashly decided golf was less painful than dentistry.

30

"I agree," I agreed, "except for one thing. I am past-tensed."

You have to protect yourself at all times when you play with Gross. This isn't meant to be funny, and I have frightening memories to prove it. So have three men who once played a round with me.

I had meant to play alone that day, concentrating on my weaknesses, in itself a lifetime job. As I walked out of the clubhouse, a friend (in the loosest possible sense) named George Smith invited me to join his threesome.

"We're playing a match," George said.

"I'm twelve," one of the others said. "What's your handicap?"

Such a question is regarded by those who know me as the punch line of a joke. Obviously I was not known to at least two of the men.

"The highest you have," I said. "Take a number."

With no apparent misgivings they accepted my word. My tee shot was to the right side of the fairway, but it was a satisfying, man-sized blow, and when I put my iron to the green and holed out in par four, the men seemed to be mumbling.

"What's this, a hustle?" I thought I heard one say to the other.

They might just as well have kept civil tongues in their heads. (And I should have kept my clubs in my bag.) It was the last hole I took. In fact it was the only hole in the entire round on which I hit a shot I'm fond of remembering. Thereafter, one experimental swing led to another tentative swipe until we came to the thirteenth.

There, as I teed up, the other three stood off to the side (as well they should have) maintaining a respectful distance and a polite silence. Suddenly the air was shattered by their terrified shrieks. Somehow, coming into the shot I'd pulled away from it slightly and toed the ball. It took off from the tee at an absolute right angle to my intended line of flight, scattering my golf mates like a covey of quail. If they'd had wings I imagine they'd have flown. Actually, it's a miracle that I missed giving at least one of them wings. I dropped two more balls, and if I had tried to do it deliberately I couldn't have repeated so accurately my first shot a second and third time. Luckily, after the first one, my companions had wisely sought sanctuary behind trees.

From there I dragged on for two more holes. On the fifteenth my tee shot skidded along the ground to my left until it met the ladies' tee marker, belting it out of the ground and 10 feet down the fairway. The ball rebounded 30 yards back over my head and fell to the thirteenth fairway of unhappy memory. I retrieved the uprooted tee marker and discovered that it had been moored into the ground with a 2-inch spike. Not even 2 inches of steel is sufficient when I'm loose. I brandished it aloft like a weight lifter. Who said I wasn't a strong hitter?

Babe Didrickson used to say that the secret of her success in golf was to loosen her girdle and let'er rip. This naturally puts a male such as myself at a distinct disadvantage, although I have been accused of going around a course as if I were dressed in a strait jacket.

One spring, while I was covering training of the major league baseball teams in Florida, my craving for golf reached a positively dangerous stage. To get my clubs in the car I had left out momma's electric blanket, her hair dryer, and a portable ironing board. But momma realized I was tottering on the brink and hoped maybe that if she left me alone I might fall over all by myself and she'd have no further problem. If you're wondering why so many things had to be left out of the trunk to pack my golf bag it's simple, although the bag is not. It sleeps six.

Many a caddy seeing this bag carried from the clubhouse, but unfamiliar with its owner, has said to himself, "This has got to be a pro. Nobody else would dare play with such plush equipment." After seeing my first few swings they know the awful truth: I'm an impostor.

Be that as it may, and usually it is, I had a date to play a round during spring training with Joe Collins, then a Yankee first baseman. I had spent days anticipating it, scheming how to steal myself and the car away from the family. Employing the most devious kind of story about sitting up with a sick infielder, I succeeded.

While I was driving out to the course, I had visions of my first shot, the ball splitting the fairway. I could almost hear Collins' envious comment, "What a belt! That'll play!" Suddenly all my first shots that would not "play": the slices . . . the hooks . . . the topped drives . . . the windies . . . flashed through my mind. I began to shake. "Will I get off? What must I remember to do? My God! I'll never hit the ball."

How could I get out of my date with Collins? Suddenly inspiration struck. I decided to make *him* not want to play. The ammunition was right at hand.

That was the day the Yankees had traded a parcel of players to the Kansas City Athletics for pitchers Bobby Shantz and Art Ditmar.

When I met Collins, he was at the first tee and eager.

"Come on," he said, "we can get right off."

"Sure," I said, with all the bravado I could muster. I let my face go bland. "By the way," I added, "have you heard about the trade?"

Collins had spent eight springs with the Yankees and was rumored to be on his way in every one of them. In fact, Joe eventually was traded, and when the Yankees let him go he quit baseball.

"Who's in it?" he asked, his knees beginning to shake in his white Bermudas.

I knew Collins' name had been kicked around in the deal, but had been withdrawn before its completion. I told him I hadn't caught the names of all the players who were sent into Siberian exile in Kansas City.

"I'd better find out," Collins said. "I can't play without

33

knowing. Maybe they're looking for me to tell me now."

All sympathy, I said, "I'll understand if you want to leave."

"Gee," said Joe, "I hate to do this, but I've just got to know."

As Collins tore off in his car, I heaved a sigh of relief, hefted the bedroom, parlor and bath I use for a golf bag and hied myself happily to the driving range.

As I have said, I make two mistakes every time I play: (1) I play with a ball, and (2) I always neglect to carry the rubber mat with me. Anyone who wants to know why I'm so much more at ease and proficient hitting off the mat than off the turf has the choice of asking my pro or my psychiatrist. (Lately the Gross family has been on an economy drive so I found a versatile fellow who could act as both.)

One afternoon at the Cherry Hills Country Club in Denver, I belted a ball as though I were angry with it and succeeded only in digging a deep and extensive divot which flew farther forward than the ball.

I walked up to that mammoth piece of mutilated sod, picked it up and turned to the caddy.

"What should I do with this?" I asked in all innocence.

"The rules say you must replace it in the hole you just dug it out of," he said. "Too bad you can't take it home and practice on it."

This was the same boy who'd lugged the bag for me a few weeks before at Cherry Hills. Halfway through the round he had developed the annoying habit of looking at his watch every few moments.

"We've got plenty of time," I protested. "Why do you keep looking at your watch?"

"This ain't a watch, mister, this is a compass." And with that he disappeared into the woods in quest of my last drive.

FOUR

○ ○ ○ ○ ○ ○ ○ ○ ○ ○

Gin and bear it

SOME of my best friends are bartenders. They are pros at their trade—good mixers, so to speak— but I wonder if they know the peculiar affinity which exists between playing golf and getting drunk, or the strange things likely to happen when you mix martinis and mashies. From personal, befuddled experience I can report what happens when you take your first shot before you reach the first tee. I can also report what happens when you stop for refills at the third, seventh, elefent and shirteensh holes. For one thing, the term "rolling green" takes on real meaning; for another the cups seem to be full up—no room for the balls. That's probably because the golfer is in *his*.

I'll always remember that day at the Engineers Club in Roslyn, New York. I was on my hands and knees in the locker room searching for a missing sock. Obviously I was undergoing my usual case of pre-round jitters, for a fellow who was getting into his clothes across from me said, "If you're looking for a sock, Mr. Gross, you've put both of them on one foot." I muttered my thanks, but was sorry I did. My new-found friend used my words of gratitude as a wedge for further social discourse. "Do you have a

36

game?" he asked. I peered at him quizzically, wondering just how I should take that question. But he seemed a nice enough fellow. He must simply have been unaware of my not easily earned reputation as the world's worst golfer.

"If you can stand playing with me," I said, giving him a fair chance to retreat with honor, "you must have the patience of a saint."

"Patience I don't have and a saint I'm not, but the cure is right here," he replied.

He reached up into his locker and produced a flask of freshly made martinis. "I know your trouble," he said. "I've seen you on the course. On the practice tee you look like a scratch golfer. On the course you tighten up. You're tense. You can't relax."

"Mister," I said, "you've just recited the sad story of my life."

"It's not sad; it's stupid," the man said. "What's so tough about this game? There's a ball and there's a club. . . ."

"Yeh," I agreed, "and then there's me."

"Right this minute we're going to start changing you," he said. He handed me the flask. "Take a belt."

That was the first. The cure consisted of repeated dosings at intervals not too distantly spaced. As I stepped to the first tee, I felt vaguely like Sam Snead's first cousin. I managed to get my drive down the middle. By the third hole I was convinced that Alcoholics Anonymous was an enemy to par shooters. By the seventh I was having trouble pronouncing Alcoholics Anonymous. By the eleventh I was having trouble pronouncing my own name. By the thirteenth I wasn't having any more trouble. I didn't remember who I was. Nor did I care.

The thirteenth at Engineers has an impenetrable jungle in a gully on the left. A tee shot must cross a ravine to land on the fairway and be playable. If there is any hole which requires concentration this is it. I was concentrating furiously. I had to. I couldn't remember teeing up more than one ball, yet as I looked down there seemed to be two, and after I blinked a few times the two seemed to have been joined by a third.

"How about that," I said. "I see more than one ball down there."

"So what," said my bibulous partner. "You got enough clubs in your hand to hit all of them."

Somehow I managed to make some kind of a connection with one of the balls. It would have been perfect if the ball were a bird seeking sanctuary in the woods, for that's where it headed. The caddy hefted the bag and started on his quest.

"Let it lay there," I called to him. "I'll take another shot instead."

"Mister," the caddy said, eying that half empty flask, "one more shot and I'll have to carry you the rest of the way. I don't mind lugging a golfer's bag, but I'll be doggoned if I'll lug a bagged golfer."

Sane golfers, of course, prefer to take their game straight and refrain from imbibing before and after they tee off. They also have the willpower to resist a recently innovated curse of the fairways—the portable bars or "watering holes" which are more challenging and fatal than any hazard yet conceived by the devilish golf course architects and engineers.

But no sooner do our soberest friends step away from the eighteenth hole, they head for the uncharted nineteenth. This is popularly known as the *master watering hole*—the oasis which offers at least temporary solace from the trials and frustrations that the golfer has just undergone. The choice and numbers of drinks usually is determined by the game a golfer played. The worse the game, the more powerful and numerous the drinks.

What the nineteenth hole proves beyond a shadow of a doubt is that the Scots invented the game solely in order to sell their national beverage in large quantities.

If this suggests that golf is some sort of a weird "never-never land," it's only because that happens to be the terrible truth. The wisest approach would seem to be to let the case rest right here, but as I've repeatedly maintained, the game isn't a game, but an addiction. There are all kinds of "pushers" seeking to lure the young and unsuspecting. They remind me of Scylla and Charybdis calling from the rocks and shoals.

I recall the time at Pine Hollow, where Bill Chadwick, the club manager, said he had a game for me with a fourteen-year-old boy.

"He hits a beautiful ball," Bill said. "You'll have a good game."

I was sure he would, but not so certain about me. As we approached the first tee, the kid kept complaining that his back was sore and his stomach upset all morning. I had been hearing the rumbling, but figured it was my own innards churning.

My beardless partner stepped to the first tee and, despite his agony, blasted a drive straight down the middle. He glared after the ball as though he were disgusted with it, but for the life of me I couldn't see a thing wrong with a shot that bisected the fairway with mathematical accuracy, some 225 yards out.

Nothing was wrong with my back as I prepared to step up to the tee. The trouble was in my head, which, after my practice swing, began to be filled with delusions of grandeur. My practice swing, as always, was smooth, rhythmical and powerful. Out of the corner of my eye, I caught the admiring glance of my youthful partner. I imagined I brought to his mind golfdom's version of Ted Williams—his gracefulness, his power, his superb coordination when he swishes his big bat back and forth as he digs in at home plate.

My first shot sent the ball from the men's tee to the ladies' tee.

"That's your mulligan," the kid said politely.

It has taken me a long time to learn the derivation of the word "mulligan" as applied to golf. It is sort of a free, for gratis, uncountable swing, which you can forget and no one will hold against you. In family-type saloons many years ago there was always a bottle called mulligan on the bar. It was as standard an item as pretzels and potato chips are today. And it was free. The basic ingredients were hot pepper seeds in water. If you were insane enough you'd swish a few drops of this devil's concoction into your beer. Chances were you'd go immediately into orbit. It ate out your liver, stomach, bladder, and finally your heart. In the psychological sense, this is precisely what happens on the tee when you accept a mulligan.

I accepted the lad's kind offer anyway but my second shot from the tee was scarcely an improvement on my first. If golf were baseball it would have been called a dribbler to the pitcher, and the only proper thing to do would have been to run it out.

"Take another shot," the kid said. "You must be a little stiff."

"You're anticipating," I said to the boy, as I turned and headed back for the locker room. "But I will be soon."

But I would hate to have people believe that all my spirits are bottled. Indeed, I have often tried in other ways to loosen the tie which binds me, bemused and benighted, to this bogeyman's game.

Last summer, for example, I pushed a shot into the lake that lines the first fairway at Fresh Meadow. As I approached the water to say the proper words of farewell over another buck and a quarter gone to its final resting place, I was struck by the beauty of a second thought. Why not take my bag, my clubs and myself and deposit all three of us in the drink? If I hung on to the bag tightly enough and resolved not to loosen my grip I would sink as quickly as my irons.

Unfortunately, the urge passed quickly, but the compulsion to give up the game permanently did not depart with the same speed. "I'll do it soon," I mumbled. "A man's got to be crazy to expose himself to this sort of torture."

There were certain amenities to be observed first, however. One was to tell the missus, who wouldn't believe it. Another was to tell my pro, Jack Oliver, who had given me the worst years of his life in a few short months.

"I won't *let* you quit," Jack said. "You swing too well not to score and once you score you'll never quit. There's got to be a gimmick."

"It's all in my head, Jack," I protested, "and unless you can arrange for a decapitation I'm afraid it's hopeless."

"It's not in your head," he insisted. "As a matter of fact all your trouble is in your legs."

Any golfer who won't listen to a pro who says he's analyzed your trouble and is willing to spend time to prove it, while all you have to expend is energy, will be haunted by what miracles *might* have occurred for the rest of his natural life. I put myself into Oliver's hands again. More accurately, I put my legs in his hands.

"Your trouble," Jack said, "is that you lock yourself at the top of your backswing. As you start down you can't get your body out of the way to let the club come through properly because you've got your left leg so tense.

"Now," he continued, "what I want you to do is to hit the ball with your left knee."

Now I'd heard everything. "I'm dying and you're kidding," I muttered.

"Who's kidding?" he answered. "I want your first movement toward the ball to be with your left knee, as though you were going to hit the ball with it."

I didn't think it would work, but it did. I was coming into the ball with the clubhead doing all the work, and there's nothing more beautiful than a shot taking off the club face before you've even realized that you've hit the ball.

"Let's go out and play the front nine," Jack said.

I could barely wait to get to the tee. My first shot split the fairway. At each shot thereafter Jack talked to me like a baby. The ball behaved magnificently. Even Ross, the caddy, who had looped for me before, alternately sneering and groaning through eighteen holes, smiled occasionally.

I was grinning broadly as I greeted my family that evening.

"You've changed your mind," my wife said. "You're not quitting."

"Honey," I said, "you won't believe this, but . . ."

She never let me finish the glorious story of that last golf lesson. She was looking at me strangely, which isn't unusual, but this was a look of indescribable curiosity.

"What's wrong with your left knee?" she asked. "Ever since you got home you've been walking around holding it funny."

"Well, that's what I've been trying to tell you." I said. "Oliver told me I had to kink that knee as I came into the ball."

"That's fine," she said, "but if you keep walking around that way with your leg held crooked, the neighbors will think you have the gout."

"As the French say," I muttered, "Chacun à son goût." Translated, this means that if you stay on the golf course and out in the open air and watch your diet at the nineteenth hole, limiting it only to scotch on the rocks and a twist of lemon peel, you'll never get gout.

FIVE

○ ○ ○ ○ ○ ○ ○ ○ ○ ○

Couch on the green

SOME YEARS AGO, Don Newcombe, who
then pitched baseballs for the Dodgers and once was sued
for pitching people out of the barroom he operated in
Newark, tried a pitch of an altogether different kind.

Newcombe astounded the baseball world by undergoing
hypnotism to cure his fear of flying. It seemed a rather
unusual approach, but Don was no more unusual than his
baseball team which had just shifted its base of operation
some 3000 miles from Brooklyn to Los Angeles. If Newcombe wanted to go along he either had to conquer the dis-
tress which plagued him each time a plane took him off the
ground, or else he had to find a new way to make a living.

Now—if I may digress for a moment in a philosophical
observation—these are Modern Times. Newcombe was apparently helped by the hypnotist and now he flies the length
and breadth of these United States. Occasionally he relaxes
even to the extent of kidding a hostess. Impressed with this
scientific cure, other baseball managers followed suit, each
in his own way. The Cincinnati Reds hired an expert rifle
shot to teach their players the art of concentration when

they were at bat. The Kansas City Apathetics hired a nutritionist to instruct their players in proper diet and table manners. Another manager, made apprehensive by the cancer-tobacco reports, plunged into a campaign to substitute bubble gum for chewing tobacco.

Who am I to turn my back on such scientific developments? If Newcombe found hypnotism to his advantage, why should I question the merits of a letter I received recently from a doctor who had read my columns on golf?

"Dear Mr. Gross," he wrote. "Your articles on your personal golf problems were quite amusing and yet very sad. I know exactly how you feel, and I imagine so do thousands of your readers. However, I'm going to relate an experience to you, which I believe you will find interesting as well as very helpful.

"I do some medical hypnosis in general practice and also on occasions I do hypnosis for entertainment purposes among friends. I have a summer home near the golf course and play there frequently.

"I have hypnotized a few caddies at the course (one of them in a shelter during a rainstorm). One caddy in particular was a favorite of the golfers. He had beautiful form on taking a practice swing, but was very tense when he played.

"It occurred to me that I could relax him under hypnosis. So, with his approval, I hypnotized him at the pro shop and gave him post-hypnotic suggestion that he would be very relaxed after he woke up, that he would play a very good game, that he would take a natural swing.

"I want to tell you that this kid played the best game of his career following this post-hypnotic suggestion. I was excited and impressed, and so was the pro. A few days later I repeated the hypnosis with the same result.

"Now here is what I would suggest to you. If there is a doctor at your club arrange to play a match with him. Ask him to hypnotize you at your home or at his office just before

46

both of you leave for the club. Have him give you the proper post-hypnotic suggestion for relaxation.

"Now, you may think this is impractical, or even impossible, but let me say that once you discover this way to relax, you will improve your game. Later you can be taught a simple but effective technique of self-hypnosis or auto-suggestion. In this day and age of 'do it yourself,' you can't afford to ignore this easy method of relaxing yourself which will guarantee that you play relaxed golf.

"Unfortunately I have not had the time to try golf hypnosis on a sufficient number of people, but I am convinced that this is the solution to your problem, and that of many others, and that it is as valuable and simple as anything you might try.

"I shall be very interested to see how hypnotism works in your particular case."

Frankly, so will I. But I haven't tried hypnotism yet and may never get around to it. If desperation and a sense of doom lead me in this direction recommended by neither the P.G.A. nor the A.M.A.—my sense of fitness leads me in the other. Somehow it seems unnatural to try to conquer this ancient game by wandering around the course directed by my subconscious mind. It is true that sometimes I wander around the course in what seems to be an unconscious state, as if I'd checked my mind with my street shoes in the locker room, but at least that's a natural condition.

I am not alone. Golf does strange things to other people, too. It makes liars out of honest men, cheats out of altruists, cowards out of brave men and fools out of everybody. Once I played with Phil Silvers, who for me is one of the funniest performers alive, but on the golf course his personality becomes as inverted as a pillow case turned inside out.

It was the ordinary sort of trying day for both of us. I sought a distraction. "Say something funny," I suggested.

"Be funny on a golf course?" he asked, clearly outraged.

"Do I kid my best friend's mother about her heart condition?"

"Okay," I said, conceding defeat. "So golf's an incurable illness."

Another time I was in the pro shop at Tamarisk in Palm Springs, California, trying to decide which of a half dozen putters I would buy to replace my old one as a rationalization for not being able to sink 2- and 3-footers. This, as all golfers know, is one of the finest outlets for evading self-recrimination. Blame it on the clubs, the ball, the weather, your companions, the atomic fallout or Khrushchev. You can also change pros like a woman changes hairdressers. So long as your dough and excuses hold out there's no need to look in the mirror and say, "It's been you all the time." Such evasion is a valuable form of therapy.

I made a discovery that day in the pro shop while vacillating among a mallet head, a blade and a cash-in rocker. Two doctors stopped in the shop prior to going out on the course. I knew of them by reputation. One was a renowned surgeon, the other a celebrated diagnostician. The surgeon was telling the diagnostician of the dreadful experience he had undergone the previous morning. He had awakened with a palsied condition in his right hand, no strength in his grip and the sensitivity gone from his fingers.

"I had to operate yesterday," he said, "and I couldn't hold the instrument steady. I had to tie off a ligature and couldn't seem to grasp it."

"That's terrible," the other said.

"What's worse," the surgeon said, "is that later in the day I came out here to play and I found I couldn't grip the clubs properly. I'm playing golf one-handed."

"I certainly appreciate how you must feel," said the diagnostician.

And how does the patient feel, I asked myself?

After this glimpse of the warping effect of golf upon the

Hippocratic oath, I've found it difficult to persuade myself to follow my benefactor's advice and be put under hypnosis. But have I arrived at some other solution? No. I have continued, doggedly and determinedly, to debase and degrade myself in a fashion that other never-will-be golfers will recognize as the norm.

For instance, in one six-week period during which I covered the spring training rituals of sixteen major league teams from Florida to Arizona, I lugged along my golf bag together with my regular luggage to the extent of $123.40 worth of excess baggage charges on cross-country planes.

As I was boarding a plane at Phoenix for Idlewild and the clerk was tallying the extra charges, another traveler in the line behind me said, "You certainly must love the game to carry your golf bag around with you."

"Mister," I answered, "I don't love the game. I hate it, but I've got to keep up appearances. The bag helps me look like the well-heeled sportsman type. And also it's a handy receptacle for dirty laundry."

I know a few men whom golf hasn't addled. My boss on the paper, Ike Gellis, is one. He is sincerely convinced that golf is man's most uplifting experience. He whistles snatches of songs as he walks the fairways in a state of blissful ignorance that he's violating one hundred different theories of the golf swing. He has the shortest backswing on record, but somehow he manages to hit a straight drive of middling distance. A dubbed shot doesn't bother him. Unconcernedly he walks to his next lie, admiring the greenery as though the last shot never happened. His mind is wiped blank of all the failures. He says a golfer must think positively and imagine himself a composite of all the great pros. He's a sort of Norman Vincent Peale of the links.

I tried to rattle him one afternoon. I reminded him that Arnold Palmer lost the 1959 Masters Tournament by failing to sink a 4-foot putt on the seventeenth and a 3-footer on the eighteenth. Jimmy Demaret, I said, knocked himself out of the possibility of becoming the first man to win the Masters four times when he hit into water on three consecutive holes.

"You miss the humor of the situation completely," Gellis chided, "and that's the trouble with your game. If you'd been looking for the light rather than the dark side you'd know what happened after Demaret finished his round."

"What happened?" I asked warily.

"Porky Oliver greeted Jimmy as he entered the clubhouse. He had a scotch on the rocks in his hand and he ran up to Demaret and asked, 'Jimmy, did you leave any water for a chaser?' "

Recently, I have been plagued by another, even higher-placed person in my hierarchy of employment. I refer to James F. Graham, a muscleman who also happens to be my managing editor and a novitiate in our set of addicts. When he told me he'd taken up the game, I sympathized with him and suggested he turn back before it was too late. When I saw that he was already hooked, I figured he wouldn't be a bad partner to play with occasionally. I could polish the apple while winning a hole now and then.

So, in the locker room and on the way to the first tee, I was all courtesy and sweetly ingratiating to him. I was ready with suggestions, advice and pleasant golfing bromides —until he hit a belt off the tee that traveled at least 250 yards straight down the middle. I stood there stunned.

I was next off. I was determined to equal his drive if I had to break my back doing it. The ball sliced off into the virgin forest as if it were a fox suddenly aware it was being chased by the hounds.

"What," I shouted in agitated despair, forgetting he was a beginner, "did I do wrong?"

"It would take less time," said Graham, with what I took to be honest confusion, "if I told you what you did right."

This is the same gentleman who, after I'd reported my effort to achieve birdies with Martinis and was considering hypnotism, came up with "Have you ever taken tranquilizer pills? They are supposed to help neurotics. Down a few just before your next round, and let me know how you make out."

I beg to differ with Mr. Graham. I'm not suffering from any deep-seated disorder. Off the golf course I'm as sweet and as even-tempered as the cow. One of my children can hold a rock-and-roll party in the house, the other can be playing cowboy with the neighborhood Indians, and I will sit pecking away at my typewriter as contentedly and unconcernedly as an infant who's just been fed and burped. But on the course, where nature and the talent of the groundskeepers are supposed to have provided a bucolic setting for my peace of mind, my nerves vibrate like the plucked strings of a bull fiddle.

Nevertheless, Graham's advice stuck in my mind. My next time out, I cadged a few Miltowns from an advertising friend, and gulped them down. As I walked through the clubhouse to get to the tee, I turned down an offer to join a threesome and an invitation for a pre-round cocktail. I didn't even want a caddy. This was to be an experiment, and I wanted to perform it myself without witnesses. As I approached the first tee, I felt relaxed and at peace with the world. When I finally addressed the ball, I was astonished. It rested serenely on the tee, and I didn't feel its mate at my throat.

At first everything went dreamily. My scorecard for the first seven holes recorded four pars and a bird. I was at ease, at complete peace with the world, lulled by the sweet and soothing sound—crack!—of clubhead meeting ball solidly. The eighth was a water hole, but that didn't bother me as it ordinarily would. This was one ball I was not going to feed to the fish. My inner conviction was such that I even dropped the ball into the washer to clean it. But suddenly my contentment was too much to bear. I yawned. I closed my eyes for a moment.

"You're tired," I told myself. "Sit down and rest a minute."

I did. I don't know how long I lay on the ground, but when I opened my eyes the sun was lower in the sky. I went back to the ball washer to retrieve my ball and continue, but the ball wasn't there. I've lost balls in every hazard and on every course on which I've tried, but when I lose a ball in the ball washer it's time to take stock.

There is an old jingle, sometimes sung in locker rooms, which goes this way:

> "See a ball and pick it up,
> All day long you'll have good luck."

That may be cricket on some courses, but it smacks of dirty pool to me. I confess that if nobody's looking, I might be tempted to sneak a lost ball off the course. But when a man's tranquilized it just doesn't seem right to go poking around in his ball washer as he lies unconscious on the ground. I applied to the house committee at my Club for a ruling on this. I'm still waiting for an answer.

Of course, my beautiful round was ruined. Man's pettiness to man had untranquilized me.

The psychological hazards of playing bad golf are formidable, but the monetary ones can be even greater. As you have no doubt guessed, I win holes infrequently.

As a workingman, I can be subject to a fairly heavy financial impost. At the club I am known as "the pigeon." Fellow members walk around with salt shakers to pour the stuff on my tail, hoping to pin me down for friendly little bets. But you'd be surprised how swiftly friendship curdles when the payments keep going one way.

One day I was brooding over the perverse twist of my fate when a player to whom I'd just lost $10, the caddy fees and the nineteenth-hole drinks thanked me for my patronage.

"Once, just once," I wailed, "I'd like to win a match from you before I die."

"Why talk about a match?" he said. "Wouldn't you be satisfied with one hole?"

"Okay," I said, "one hole."

"Milt," the ungrateful cad said, "that will be your consolation when you die. They'll bury you in a hole that will be yours and nobody else's."

Another friend who had played with me enough to know it wasn't worth the agony just to win a few bucks listened to the colloquy and added his dissent.

"No," he said, "you'll never be buried, Milt. It just wouldn't be fitting for you to be in one place. They should cremate you and scatter your ashes over the course. Then when the wind blows, everybody will know that things still are the same. 'There goes Gross all over the place again,' they can say."

SIX

○ ○ ○ ○ ○ ○ ○ ○ ○ ○ ○

No laughing matter

AT THE FIRST TEE Jackie Gleason was pacing back and forth impatiently waiting for Ike Gellis and me. The date had been set for 8 A.M., but at 7:45 TV's fat and funny man already was taking his practice swings. The dew was heavy on the grass and over the Pocono Mountains the mist had not been completely evaporated by the sun, but Gleason had been up before the sun and there was no holding him.

"Come on, come on," Jackie urged. "We'll never get in fifty-four if we don't hurry."

"Fifty-four what?" I asked, weakly.

"Holes," Jackie screamed, every inch of his amplitude aquiver with impatience. "What do you think? Eighteen before breakfast, eighteen before lunch and eighteen after lunch."

"Who eats lunch?" I said, overwhelmed by the ambitious program which had been laid out for me behind my back. I realized once again that when you play golf with a comedian, you should not expect comedy.

My suspicions were confirmed when only recently Leonard Lyons asked Bert Lahr, one of the old-time comics, to explain the difference between comedians of his day and those of the present day. The questioner anticipated a learned discussion on the elements of humor, but instead Lahr answered in one word: "Golf."

When you team up, as I have, with Gleason, Buddy Hackett, Phil Silvers, Jerry Lester, Alan King or Milton Berle, the fairways might just as well be dotted with tombstones, mortuaries and mausoleums, it's that quiet and eerie. It must be the game that does it to them. There just isn't a gag in a bagful once the ball is on the tee and the club is in their hand. Their humor curdles, and the cream of the country's jokesters become the sourpusses of the land.

Of course, without their gag writers many comedians would be struck dumb, but the austerity of golf does something to them that a psychiatrist would have trouble explaining.

Once I played a round with Jerry Lester at the Normandie Golf Club in St. Louis. Lester missed a putt that would have given him a par. His try for a bogey was on a downhill lie. He tapped the ball carelessly. It gathered speed, hit the edge of the green, rolled over the apron and into a trap. By the time the ball had stopped moving, Lester had torn his scorecard into little pieces and strewn them over the green. He flung his putter into the sand and was about to fling himself into the pit when I asked the caddy, "Was this green cut this morning?"

"Yes, sir," he said hesitatingly, obviously appreciating, as I did not, that there is a time for play and a time for work.

"Be specific," I said. "At what time?"

From the bottomless pit Lester reared his head, bared his teeth and growled, "Who the hell's writing your lines?"

Another comedian, Jackie Miles, once spoke wisely to me of golf. I saw him one night doing his turn in Las Vegas, where the Desert Inn's course offers a temporary respite from the dice and roulette tables. There a man has

ample opportunity to decide which is the more deadly and trying on a man's nerves and pocketbook. The dice and wheel offer mathematically calculated risks. Golf is beyond calculation.

Miles saw me at a ringside table and winked. In pantomime I suggested a date the following day for a round of golf.

"Who plays golf any more?" Miles said. "I've gone in for gambling now. At the tables I only lose my money. On the course I lose my mind."

It turned out that he didn't own clubs any more. "I took them to the casino," he explained, "and use them for croupier's sticks. I got a better chance of cashing in at the tables."

Miles is an exception. The rest of the nation's comics seem as naturally attracted to the stultifying game as the moth is to the flame.

Phil Silvers tried to explain the perverse pull of the game to me one day, after he'd persuaded his wife, the beautiful Evelyn Patrick, that I wanted to interview him for a column. I did, in a way, but the notes were taken between strokes.

"I pulled the same fraud with *my* wife," I told Silvers. "I told her I had a date to talk to you. How crazy can we be? Neither one of us is having fun. We're both hacking up the real estate, and I'm afraid my caddy is going to drop my bag and walk out on me. Why? Why do we punish ourselves?"

"I'll tell you about this game," Silvers said, as he gently picked at his ear with a tee. It struck me that the tee in the ear was serving a more salutary purpose than it was when stuck in the ground. At least he was improving his hearing.

"Aren't we lucky out here in the open air away from the smoke of night clubs and such?" he said. "So we worry about playing a good game. That's all right. When I worry about other things, the only exercise I get is pacing up and down in a stuffy room. For a few hours a day, I can have

59

a happy worry with golf. I can worry healthily and out of doors."

Jackie Gleason has become obsessive about golf. He would play around the clock, if it were possible. Actually, this is to be expected because Jackie doesn't do anything by halves. When he built a new home in Peekskill, New York, he just didn't contract for one house; he had the contractor build a second beside the first to handle whatever overflow of guests happened along.

"I couldn't believe it," said Harry Obitz, at Shawnee, where Jackie discovered golf in June, 1957. "The other day he teed off at 8 A.M. and was in at 11 A.M.

" 'Did you play the full eighteen?' I asked Jackie.

" 'Hell,' he said, 'I've gone thirty-six.' I'd never seen anybody play thirty-six holes in three hours before."

Jackie has worn out several electric carts and a caddy named Dusty. Playing with a form and style that would make a purist ill, Gleason rushes up to the ball, glances down at it, swipes at it, climbs into the electric cart and rushes after the ball. Behind him Dusty lopes likes a trained bird dog. After Jackie holes out, Dusty tees up the next ball for him. At the end of the day Gleason is as fresh as a new joke and impatient for morning to come around again. Dusty and the electric cart sag a bit.

Those with whom Gleason plays also seem the worse for wear. For one thing, Jackie's mathematics on the course are somewhat faulty. There was one hole, I remember, in which Jackie was knee-deep in rough, and I still recall my vivid impression that he was using the wrong club when he pulled a 4-wood from the bag to extricate himself. What he needed from that lie was a bulldozer. The thought was followed by a second impression that Gleason had taken a couple of swings at the ball which still lay there contentedly in its hideout despite the whistling of the wind around it. After the hole had been completed and Jackie announced his score, there appeared to be a couple of strokes missing.

"Don't worry about them," said Ike Gellis, whose view-point about golf is so broad it has earned him a reputation as a humanitarian. "All you heard were echoes, not strokes." For another thing, Gleason is what somebody once called "a floating hazard." He has a fine disregard for what is known as golfing etiquette. Naturally, this does not imply that a man is unmannerly if he is profane, throws one club, recklessly, breaks another, and cusses out the caddy. In fact, some of the most mannerly men I know have wrapped their clubs around trees in the most genteel sort of way.

One man in particular comes to mind as an illustration of what delightful people you meet on the golf course. He is a hotel magnate named Joe Wolf, who was building a multimillion dollar motel in Phoenix, Arizona, called the Caravan Inn. He suggested a game one day and was the perfect host. He provided all the equipment and clothes and even drove us out to the Phoenix Country Club.

One thing Joe could not provide was direction for his drives. When two of them went into the drink at a water hole, Joe calmly asked the caddy for his bag. He lifted it himself, traipsed up to the pond, took the bag from his shoulder, and heaved it into the water. Then he turned and walked off the course while the rest of us stood in discreet, respectful and appropriate silence.

Joe hadn't gone a hundred yards when he turned and came slowly back toward us. He went directly to the pond, carefully removed his shoes and socks, turned up his trouser legs, and waded in to retrieve the bag. He unzipped a pocket carefully, searched inside and pulled out the keys to his car. Then he rezipped the compartment just as care-fully and tossed the bag back into the water.

"You'll have to pardon me," he said. "For the moment I'd forgotten I must drive you back."

Gleason, on the other hand, never drove me anywhere, except mad. Honors mean nothing to Jackie. Nor do the rules of traffic that dictate that whoever is away is up first.

No sooner does Jackie swing than he is off after his ball, with Dusty pointing out the direction, leaving the rest of us to wait until he is safely out of harm's way before teeing off. On the green Jackie's impatience leads him to hole out before anybody else has a chance to line up a putt properly.

You have to take all this in good grace, though, when Jackie explains his feeling for the game he had adopted as though he'd invented it. "This is the greatest," Gleason exults. "What a way to relax! Before this I used to get no exercise except for the walk from the bar to the men's room in Toots Shor's."

It is well known that a man would take with more tolerance a slur at his masculinity, disparagement of his ancestry and even a down-rating of his credit standing before he would accept any insulting insinuations about his golf.

When he is alone with himself, his conscience and whatever deities there be who control the vagaries of this ridiculous game, a golfer may admit that possibly, just possibly, he falls short of being the image of a Ben Hogan. However, within himself there is that ever-present germ of a dream (some call it a delusion) that he is on the threshold of mastering himself and his clubhead. Over the next bunker lies the Eden of every golfer.

Otherwise, why do the duffers go on punishing themselves on the rack of impossible desire, remembering the fleeting moments when balls went straight and far for some inexplicable reason. It is like a reverie of youth returning after libido had fled. It is the hallucination that makes us kings for the fleeting moment when we will not see that we are clothed in rags. Walter Mitty was an unimaginative clod compared to the duffer who longs to recapture that rare, irretrievable round when he, the club and the ball operated together as the devil intended.

Before me, as I relive such a moment, is a scorecard, dog-eared and thumb-printed—also attested, certified, and notarized. So long as I retain this memento of one blessed day in a lifetime of grief, I know I will never consign my clubs to the attic. It is my uplift. I have ogled this scorecard with more desire than I would Miss America. We duffers cling to straws that a drowning man would disdain. He goes down only three times. There is no limit to the number of times a golfer will fan the dead embers of his hopes back to glowing life.

The thought is a simple one and always the same: *If I almost did it once, I could almost do it again*. It is the last good shot after a hundred bad ones which brings you back again to the torture chamber. The afternoon which the scorecard represents I shot a 48 for nine at the Detroit Golf Club. In itself this may not be remarkable, but I got it while three-putting nine greens.

My friends, who thought I was merely resorting to the prerogative of all duffers to bend the truth a bit, have had that scorecard thrust into their faces with the heated reminder that if I had managed to two-putt the greens—gad! The thought is just too wonderful to contemplate.

As the last putt was sunk and the card tallied, I grabbed my partners by their shirts, pushed pencils into their hands and insisted that they attest the score. I was disturbed, of course, because we had no more time to play a second nine but more so because there were no photographers around. Still, I carry around in my head even today scenes from that glorious round.

Earlier in the round, with a stiff wind bringing tears to my eyes, the caddy advised that I couldn't get home with my first shot off the fairway.

"Play it safe," he said, "and then pitch to the green."

"My three wood," I said, with all the iciness I could put into my voice, "and then get the putter ready."

Oh, the memory of that blow. The ball fairly spit into the face of the wind and made the green. What difference, if I needed three putts to find the hole? There'd been so many other days when it still took three after taking six to get that far.

Another round I remember vividly, at least in part, took place at North Hills in Douglaston, New York. My partner was Lester Scott, the Madison Square Garden publicist, who looks less like a golfer than Little Orphan Annie and plays better than most amateurs dare hope. I don't play with Scotty any more. I'm willing, but he has a squeamish streak in his medicine ball body. He says he wouldn't want to be there the next time I threaten to cut my throat.

On the first seven holes I stayed out of trouble with miraculous regularity and was only a couple of strokes over par. On the seventh I put a fairway wood to the green, a putter's length from the cup, which brought an exclamation from Scott that rings in my ear with the beauty of a church bell even at this date.

"Snead couldn't have hit that ball better," he said.

Thus we came to the eighth. We couldn't play the regular tee, which was being resodded. Some cretin of a groundskeeper had installed a temporary tee on a mat sunk into the ground, only the grooves in the mat faced directly toward an out-of-bounds fence.

As a lefthander, that faced me too much to the right. I compensated, or maybe I overcompensated, and my drive hooked over the fence. The second shot, after I carefully rearranged my hands on the club, dropped into a gully on the left. The third somehow went from the temporary tee to the regular tee. In blind exasperation I rushed at the ball and was about to swing at it furiously when the groundskeeper came running up.

"You can't drive from there," he shouted. "That's under repair."

"For your information," I screamed at him, "this is not my drive; it's my third shot."

SEVEN

○ ○ ○ ○ ○ ○ ○ ○ ○ ○

His course is his castle

OLD BLUES who have bled red on the Yale University golf course remember with a mixture of kindliness and chagrin the benefactor who made the course possible and also a little impossible.

The benefactor was an alumnus who left a $200,000 endowment to the university with the specific provision that it be spent on the construction of a golf course. Andrew Carnegie is reputed to have said that golf is the "indispensable adjunct to high civilization" and maybe that's where this well-heeled Yalee got the idea. I have heard other, less favorable descriptions of the sport and some of them have been voiced on the Yale course about that generous alumnus. He had qualified his beneficence with another stipulation. Each hole had to be designed to try men's souls, otherwise there would be no money and no course.

Yale complied. There are Old Blues who have tested the course and haven't been heard from since the raccoon coat and bathtub gin era. The expression "23-Skidoo" has its origins here. It means the number of strokes you usually take on the first hole before you get lost permanently.

This is the course where a friend of mine came out to

play with two dozen balls and tapped out on the ninth hole, which requires a 175-yard carry over a lake onto a green the size of a bottle cap. Reggie Root, the former Eli football coach, considered himself something of a golfer until the day he hit four straight balls into the water on the 9th. He teed up the fifth ball, with somewhat less confidence. His drive carried to the lake again.

"Did that one go in, too?" he called to the caddy.

"I think so, sir," the caddy answered, obviously estimating that his answer should not be too positive.

"Let's take a look and be sure," Root said.

He strode up to the pond in time to watch the fading of the last ripple where his fifth shot had landed. He stretched out his hand to the boy.

"Do you want to drop a ball?" the boy asked.

"I do not," said Root." I want to drop my bag." He did just that—in the lake—and never played golf again. It is a Yale alumnus of deepest azure, Bob Cooke, the former sports editor of the *New York Herald Tribune* and now a radio sportscaster for CBS, who tells the story but he always adds: "And we wouldn't want to change a blade of grass on the course, much less the hazards."

I've a sneaking suspicion that Yale must own stock in every company which manufactures golf balls. There is only one other explanation for such deluded devotion, and it is endemic with all golfers who belong to golf clubs. Ask any duffer about his club, and he'll tell you his is the best. He may have left a trail of broken clubs and lost balls from the first to the eighteenth. It may be a dreadful place, but he loves it. The fairways may be planted with chickweed, but he'll tell you the greens are real tricky. The terrain he traverses up and down may be fit for only mountain goats, but he'll tell you it sure is a sporty course, isn't it. He thinks of his club the way he thinks of his parents.

Even members of the Pine Valley Golf Club in New

Jersey praise it in the warmest terms until they break down and admit that in the privacy of their clubhouse they often refer to it as "the Valley of Despair." Pine Valley was hacked out of the wilderness in southern New Jersey, approximately 15 miles from Philadelphia, and if you crawled on your hands and knees from the city of Brotherly Love to the first tee it wouldn't be more arduous than hiking over the course itself.

An average golfer who has never played Pine Valley before should be forewarned about it: Bring balls, lots of them! When he arrives at the club he is invited to make a sporting wager—a five-dollar bet that he does not break 100 the first time around.

Eugene Storey, the British golfer, was invited to play the course. He was delighted both with the invitation and the challenge. All went well for the first hole, but when Storey reached the second tee he rubbed his eyes in disbelief at what he saw.

The green was 353 yards away, but uphill from tee to flag. Interlocked traps guarded the green like so many Horatios at the bridge and to get there the hitter must not falter even once. Between the tee and the first trace of a green fairway lay a 150-yard yawning trap, which has been known to capture a player and never release him.

"Interesting, interesting," said Storey to his host. "But tell me one thing. Do you play this hole or merely photograph it?"

But the world offers the golfing connoisseur many courses more hazardous and exotic even than Pine Valley. For instance, in far-off British East Africa, there is the Nyanza Club on Lake Victoria. One of the local hazards produced the following regulation: "If a ball comes to rest in dangerous proximity to a hippopotamus or crocodile, another ball may be dropped at a safe distance, no nearer to the hole, without penalty."

In India, the Bombay Presidency Golf Club, Limited, warns its members: "The area known as The Elephant Pit is a hazard whether or not it contains water."

Likewise at the Darwin Golf Club, Australia: "Ball may be lifted and dropped without penalty from Wallaby and Bandicoot Scrapes, Crab Holes, Stone Outcrops and Genuine Earth Cracks."

At the Bolarum Golf Club in Hyderabad, India, a rule reads: "A ball lying on any of the footpaths, cutcha roads, cattle and cart marks or dung on the course, may be lifted and dropped without penalty."

The closest I've ever come to a crocodile was a family of alligators which lived in a water hole on a course in Tarpon Springs, Florida, and operated on the principle that its home was its castle. I was invited by a Southern friend to team up with him on the course. It was pleasant enough, if I disregarded the sand fleas which made an eighteen-course meal of my legs, the moles that ate their way through the fairways, and the alligator that yawned at the caddy.

My friend was having a bad day. At the alligator hole he raised the water level with a half dozen balls, stubbornly refusing to forfeit a stroke and drop one at the near side of the hole. When he ran through all his balls, he ordered the caddy into the pond. The caddy obediently waded in, but no sooner had he stirred up the water when a resting 'gator lifted its head, casually slid from its perch under a cypress tree and glided slowly and malevolently from the shore into the pond. The caddy beat a hasty retreat, while the man said: "In this club a caddy's supposed to retrieve a ball if a member tells him to. I'm going to report you to the caddy master."

"Don't do that, Mister," the caddy pleaded. "I want to keep on caddying. My daddy caddied here. Wait till that 'gator goes back to sleep again and I'll fetch you your balls."

"That's more like it," said my Southern friend. We sat

69

beneath a tree waiting for the alligator to doze (it was the most leisurely eighteen I ever played) and the alligator and I must have dropped off at about the same time. Anyway, when they shook me awake, the caddy had retrieved the balls and my friend was ready to start hitting them into the lake again.

With all this rich experience behind me as to the willingness of the devoted golfer to put up even with the sleeping habits of alligators if need (or the cost of balls) dictated, I should not have been chagrined a couple of summers ago to have received an indignant letter from a reader who took exception to some of my remarks made in print about the course in Honesdale, Pennsylvania.

What my critic did not understand was that I wasn't knocking the course so much as I was knocking myself. Art Wall, the Masters winner in 1959, happens to hail from Honesdale. Appreciating that when a man's going badly he can't just blame it on himself, Art readily understood my column. A golfer might as well turn in his clubs if he can't find some excuse for his own duffery.

When you're not even getting off the tee, you can't possibly harbor kind thoughts about the course that's defeating you. But at Honesdale, even stranger things were taking place. While my tee shots were doing nothing for me (the ball usually rolling a few yards off the tee) my second shots, 3-wood usually, were booming. I switched from the driver to the 3-wood for the remaining tee shots but still experienced the same trouble. I just couldn't hit the ball more than a rolling distance from the tee, but my second shot invariably took off for the green, even though I was using the same club for both. I began to think the Honesdale tees didn't like me.

Subsequently, writing in the *New York Post,* I commented calmly on what had occurred. Among other things, I painted this pleasant bucolic picture of the Honesdale Course: "A sort of pasture on which despairing humans

70

rather than cows wander determinedly, if aimlessly, ankle deep in dandelions which pass for fairway grass."

No offense meant, of course, but not too long afterward I received a letter and an enclosure from Ed Weiner, a former N.Y.U. football player and now Broadway press agent. The enclosure was a letter addressed to Weiner by one Hamilton Federman of Honesdale. It read: "Dear Ed, Enclosed please find the clipping that many of the people in Honesdale have not been pleased to read. Perhaps many great golfers have not praised this course, but few have been in a position to put it into print. Now along comes a guy who instead of giving it a line or two of praise slaps the course down. After so many years of playing this course this article must get you stirred up."

Weiner's covering letter said: "You wrote a whole me-gillah [a lot] about the golf course at Honesdale. In other words, after rapping the nine-hole layout you also claimed you were hitting the ball straight and were splitting the pins.

"The citizens of Honesdale are up in pitchforks at your article slurring their golfing paradise.

"For the last fifteen years I've played that course and every time I toured the nine holes it reaffirmed the feeling within that some day I may still conquer the game of golf. I average thirty-five strokes for the nine. This cannot be said of any other course I've played. And you! You have the audacity to rap my little Shangri-la. You have Gross-ly maligned an innocent pasture.

"You also write of your and others' frustrations with the good old Scotch game, but why do you penalize a layout where you play? This course is an antidote, an elixir superior to wonder drugs, for the sick golfer, into whose ranks you have inducted yourself.

"Please, Mr. Gross, don't take my medicine away from me. You play your course and I'll play mine. You can still repent by saying in print, 'Honesdale has a nice course.' "

To the citizens of Honesdale, Pennsylvania: Honesdale is a nice course. And so is Aldercress, the Yolo Flier's Club in California, the U.S. Naval Ammunition Depot Course in the Canal Zone, and many another club whose fairways I have yet to fertilize. Such filial devotion does my heart good. It also proves that fairways not only can grow grass but the oddest, most devoted breed of men and women ever turned out of a pro shop. The attachments one forms at a golf club are gordian knots which bind you to your Sleepy Pines, Weeping Willows, Burning Trees, and Glen Oaks. Woodman, spare that tree, or suffer the wrath of its membership, which is like no wrath ever wrought.

Although the love of a golfer for his course is invariably blind, the love of a house owner whose castle is adjacent to the links can easily be turned to hate. A recent case before the New Jersey State Supreme Court was won by Mr. and and Mrs. Ralph Sans of Ramsey, New Jersey. The couple had sued the Ramsey Golf and Country Club to limit its playing hours or alter its third tee. Victory was not won, however, until the case had dragged on for four years, through three courts, and the Sanses had sold their home and moved to a new one twelve miles away.

Mr. and Mrs. Sans in the legal sense were the plaintiffs but actually they were the defendants. And they were tired of defending themselves against flying missiles. They had purchased their home from the National House and Farms Association, which had created the country club as part of a housing development. The Sanses were members of the club.

However, the club encroached a little too personally and geographically on their property. Their back yard was a few feet from a lake, which formed the hazard of the club's third hole. The third tee was practically in their back yard. Three windows faced the fairway and water hazard. When Justice John J. Francis ruled the tee a "nuisance to home-

72

owners," he enjoined club members from using it. When the club was ordered to move its third tee to the other side of the pond, thus eliminating the drive across the water, the rules committee objected. It held that an attractive short par-four water hole would become transformed into an ordinary par-three hole on a nine-hole course which already had three par three's.

However, said Justice Francis, speaking for the court's 6-0 decision, it would be "manifestly incompatible with the ordinary and expected comfortable life" of the Sans family to allow the situation to continue as it had.

Until that point the Sans' life had been somewhat hectic, according to Justice Francis's comments. "The constant movement of the players to and from the tee in close proximity to their rear lawn and house was accompanied by a flow of conversation which became annoying and burdensome to them.

(*"Fore!"*)

"It awakened them and their children as early as seven in the morning and it pervaded their home all day long until twilight.

(*"Mommy, wake up. There's a golfer in your petunia bed."*)

"Occasionally a low hook or slice or heeled shot of a golfer carried upon their lawn. Then, by means of a trespass, the ball is retrieved. Sometimes it is played from that position.

(*"Look at the boob, dear, using a seven iron from behind the garage. The last trespasser to try it broke our—" Crash!*)

"While silence is the conventional courtesy when a golfer is addressing his ball and swinging, the ban is relaxed between shots, and presumably the nature of the comments depends in some measure upon the success or failure of the player in negotiating the hazardous water."

(*"Why in —— I ever took up this —— game I'll never know!"*)

73

Justice Francis went on to reveal that a golfer once told the Sans children to quiet their dog. When they didn't, he kayoed the pup with his 7-iron.

If the Sans family was just a little more psychiatrically attuned to golfing diseases, they would understand that these golfers are more to be pitied than censured. They are afflicted with a not uncommon ailment, namely, aquaphobia. You can drink water, swim in it, wash in it, race boats in it, and use it to dilute whiskey, but when it comes to hitting a golf ball over it, H_2O becomes something else again. For one thing it seems to have a magnetic attraction for golf balls. For another, it repels most golfers in such a way their nervous systems become affected.

Perhaps the Sans père, mère or fils were also concerned that some morning they'd find a body floating within sight of their kitchen window, and this is no way to start the day. Possibly, in eliminating the water hole at Ramsey, the court considered its action not only as justice to the plaintiff but in the common good.

If more courts took this keen an interest in golfing problems, possibly we wouldn't have to contend with such hellish holes as the sixteenth at Cypress Point in California, a 240-yard par-three which is a peninsula sticking out into the Pacific Ocean. Foaming breakers smash themselves on the rocks which frame the green. Out of bounds is the ocean. In the 1952 Bing Crosby Pro-Amateur Tournament, Lawson Little took a 14 and Henry Ransom an 11 on this hole.

If you can live through Cypress Point, then you must surely expire on the eighteenth at Pebble Beach, a mile and a half away. I wouldn't try to play the course, much less describe it. But another newspaperman did, and his description only can be classified as diabolically apt. Wrote the late Howard Vincent O'Brien of the Chicago *Daily News* about Pebble Beach:

"I dragged my aching calves through the tortuous maze of the world-famous Pebble Beach course—one of the four eighteen-hole soul wreckers in the Del Monte properties.

"I played with the great Lawson Little—'with' in the sense that we were on the fairway at the same time. Or, to be even more accurate, while *he* was on the fairway and I was out in the Pacific Ocean with the seals.

"This is a great course to have played; but in this world, tremulous with uncertainty, I cling happily to the immutable fact that I shall never have to undergo such an ordeal again.

"The architect of Pebble Beach must have derived his inspiration from Dante's account of a trip through hell. And he added terrors never dreamed of by the Italian poet.

"Most of the fairway—itself hardly wider than the seat in a Pullman diner—winds along cliffs high above the sea, boiling in angry foam among the rocks far below.

"In addition to the normal golfing hazards of hook, top and slice, the player on Pebble Beach must have the nerves of a steeplejack. To give you an idea of the terrain, just imagine yourself trying to execute a brassie shot from a lie on a cornice of the Empire State Building, with a 40-mile-an-hour gale wrapping a bundle of fog around your head.

"At one spot along the precipice I saw a rude wooden cross. I was told that this marked the spot where a player had lost his last ball, and where, after tossing his clubs, one by one, to Neptune, had himself dived to happy oblivion. He had played only four holes, but they had been enough.

"The one bright feature of my hours on Pebble Beach, as a combination of duck, chamois and sea gull, was that I forgot deadlines, income tax, the problems of child psychology and all other afflictions of normalcy. At the end, it was enough that I had survived."

Sometimes a golf course is a real threat to the survival of those passing casually by. Bob Mardian, an attorney-at-law in Pasadena, California, vouched for the following case in point one evening with his right hand held high and

a glass in it. A freeway, which is a California equivalent of a speedway, runs along the fourth and fifth holes of the Annandale Country Club in Pasadena. It was there that a golfer drove off the tee, but sliced the ball so severely that it hit the window of a car, smashed the window and hit the driver. The car jumped the freeway, killed twelve people and injured thirteen. The police, called to the dreadful accident, tracked down the man who hit the ball.

The crowd, which had gathered in macabre curiosity, mumbled angrily about what a dreadful thing it is to have a golf course paralleling a highway.

"What's so terrible about it?" the golfer demanded.

"Good God, man, don't you know what you've done?" a cop said.

"Sure, I do," the golfer said. "If I had closed up my stance a little and followed all the way through that ball would have gone straight down the middle and I wouldn't have sliced at all."

EIGHT

o o o o o o o o o

Anything you can do he can do better

THE KIND OF GAME golf has become these days it is possible to find anything on the course, including the bleached white bones of the combatants, discarded girdles, broken-down helicopters, escaped inmates from nearby asylums, and grumbling, malevolent caddies who are sure they can play better than the players (in my case they're right) and don't mind letting them know it.

In some country clubs, caddies have become virtually extinct. Automation, in the form of battery-driven caddy carts, have taken their place. Other courses are equipped with pushcarts. These have the virtue of being speechless, sneerless and tipless. They lack personality, however. Without them, golf is like a platonic relationship with Sophia Loren or drinking caffein-free coffee. It may be painless, but it's not so challenging as traversing a course under a broiling sun with a surly bag-toter pantomiming his disgust at your wild shots.

I remember the caddy who toted for me through eighteen long holes at Baltusrol in Springfield, New Jersey. "I've gone off my game completely," I said. "I can't figure out what I'm doing."

"Mister," he said, "you're doing one thing when you should be doing another."

"What are the two things?" I asked.

"You're choking when you should be stroking," he said.

The caddy escaped without being clipped with a cleek, perhaps because it was a moment of truth.

When you allow a caddy to tote your bag, you've virtually invited him to share your soul. If he needles you on every stroke and every hole with his acid comments and despairing facial expressions, intimidates you into using the club you don't want to use, pockets your lost ball which he later tries to sell back to you, takes credit for your good shots and disassociates himself completely from your bad ones, there is nothing you can blame but tradition.

Although history is almost as fuzzy as some caddies (who somehow manage to be stewed by 8 A.M. tee-off time), we are told that the caddy came into being after James I, the Scottish king, declared golf to be the royal game in the fifteenth century. A king couldn't be expected to pack his own clubs, and the palace lackeys were assigned to the chore. A lackey who regularly did light duty around the royal ranch was known as a cadet, and the Scots eventually twisted the term into "cadee." The only reason I would doubt this version of the origin of the caddy is that if caddies then were as they are now most of them would have had their heads cut off by royal decree.

The caddy today has the edge from the moment he totes your bag. Under a caddy's withering glance, I have even approached the starter's table with an inferiority complex, before I've as much as swung at the ball. You pay him, but he's your boss and severest critic. When he's assigned to you, he's probably been called from a hot roll in the dice game which goes on permanently in the caddy shed. Chances are he's already been tipped off about your idiosyncrasies by another caddy, about the magnetic attraction of your ball for the woods and streams, and about

your conformist tendencies in sticking to the club rule which specifically states you must not spoil a caddy for the other members by tipping him over the regular fee.

Overtipping can happen, of course, and it was done to extremes when Frank Costello, that well-heeled man about the Mafia, played the old Bayside Club in Queens, New York. A caddy looping for the gang overlord, who played a regular daily round before stray gunmen began taking pot shots at him and the government started deportation proceedings, knew he was going to be tipped a fresh, crisp $100 bill.

Soon a situation developed at Bayside in which caddies would hide from regular members, who tipped somewhat more sensibly. When Costello showed, so did all the caddies. The leftovers, assigned to other golfers without jail records and in the lower income brackets, spent the remainder of the day mumbling about their bad luck and the cheapskates they had to loop for.

Eventually the club had to take measures to stop the disappearing acts by its caddies. As diplomatically as possible, Costello was told to pick a boy who could caddy for him permanently, so the other members could be assured of a game at any time. The arrangement went well until one day Costello saw a new boy coming for his bag.

"Where's Diamond Jim?" asked Costello, referring to his caddy by the name the other caddies had tagged on him in his affluence.

"Boss," the new caddy said, "You ain't got Diamond Jim no more. I won you from him in the crap game."

Going out to play a round is like a crap game in a way if a caddy's going to carry your bag. You never know what kind of a number is coming up—young, old, fat or skinny, talkative or morose, a help or a hindrance, polite or as sympathetic as a fox in a hen house. One thing you can be sure of. No serpent's tooth was ever sharper than a caddy's tongue.

I once played the treacherous and deceptive course at the Southern Hills Country Club in Tulsa, Oklahoma. The fairway seemed to be no wider than a subway aisle. It was a long day for me. It must have been longer for the caddy, who looked as though he weren't enjoying himself at all.

"This is the toughest course I've ever played," I alibied, aware that my bag wasn't exactly a paper sack, and that I was taking the long way home. A pedometer would have proved I had lengthened the course to thrice what the architect intended.

"Where that green stuff is," said the caddy, "that's the course. You haven't been on it since the first tee."

"You haven't exactly been a help," I said.

"You want help, go see the pro," the caddy said. "I'm lugging your clubs because I need the money, but if I ever get out of this rough they'd have to fill your bag with ten-dollar bills for me to loop for you again."

My inclination was to retort—uh—sharply, but I've learned through bitter experience that caddies don't chide duffers for the fun of it. Frequently they undergo severe physical and mental ordeals.

I've known caddies named Chicago, King Farouk, Red Dog, Dim Wit, and Dumb Dan. Dumb Dan deliberately took his name under false colors. He pretended to be a mute and in this cleverly developed sanctuary he never had to talk to the players or answer when they asked, "What am I doing wrong?" His masquerade had to be dropped one afternoon when he no longer could resist the temptation to jab in his needle.

His player had sliced nine consecutive balls out of bounds over a fence which ran parallel to the fairway.

"Dammit, that's enough," the player swore. "If I can't get one ball on the fairway in nine I ought to quit."

Dumb Dan broke the sulphurous silence which followed.

"Don't quit now," he mumbled, more to himself than to the other. "Lose three more. Cheaper by the dozen."

This might pass for sympathy coming from a caddy who seems congenitally unable to utter a kind syllable without wielding the needle. Of course, he's not born caustic. He just assimilates his nastiness passing his time with one hacker after another who rarely can find a kind word to say about himself except on that rare, rare day when he is playing up to his unusual game.

Even the young caddies get under your skin more quickly than their years warrant. Flub two holes and they either snicker or offer advice. They mean no harm, but they've picked up a few phrases and a few mannerisms from the veteran sneerers in the caddy shed.

One little freckle-faced urchin proved an exception. He had a warmer smile than you'd expect to find on the face of anyone lugging seventy pounds on his back. The boy carried for me, a lefthander, and my opponent, a right-hander, and both of us sliced. The kid's tongue was hanging far enough out of his mouth to be sunburned. Nevertheless, every time he came up to either of us, his speckled kisser shone as if his job were a joy to him, pure and un-diluted.

On one par-four hole particularly, the kid seemed to have become part of me. My drive was right down the middle. My second shot hit the green with just the correct amount of backspin. My first putt left the ball in fine position for a par, but it must have been too much for my duffer's nature. The ball slid by the cup on the next putt.

On the drive Freckles applauded eagerly. *"We* sure belted that one!" he crowed. On the approach he cried hap-pily, *"We're* home! *We're* home!" On the first putt he said, "Now *we'll* sink the next one for *our* par." As the ball missed the cup, there was not only shame, but disgust on his freckled puss. Suddenly we had lost our unity. *"You* sure blew that one," he moaned.

Theoretically, this is the way it should be. The caddy, for the time it takes to traverse eighteen holes, becomes the teammate and confidante of the player. You don't expect undying loyalty, but there should be a measure of fealty, whether it's born of the misspent hours together or the anticipation of the rich reward the player passes to the caddy.

An example of undying loyalty was the late Joe Horgan, to whom the United States Golf Association officially presented credentials as the dean of American caddies. Horgan became enamored of Henry Vardon, the Englishman, and would regale other caddies, as well as players and pros, with his favorite's virtuosity. One pro for whom Horgan was looping, got himself trapped during a tournament but hit a remarkable recovery dead to the pin.

"What do you think of that shot?" the pro asked Horgan. "Could Vardon have got out the way I did?"

"Got out?" Horgan snorted. "Mr. Vardon never would have been in."

The years, perhaps, have thinned out the strain of such caddies as Joe Horgan. To him it was a life's work, a profession in which he prided himself, a heritage from the ancient Scots, who, of course, got their caddies free. The Scots broke in youngsters who wanted to become pros. In the process of their training the boys caddied for their teachers.

Oh, for the days of the gutta-percha ball and the twenty-five-cent round. Today we lose buck-and-a-quarter balls and feel inferior to caddies who turn their back or turn up their lip at anything less than five bucks a round. But I shouldn't complain. My caddy always earns his fee. And invariably he is better at his task on the links than I am at mine.

Like many fine golfers, Jimmy Demaret began his golf career as a caddy, and today supports so many of them. His annual expenditure for caddy fees along the tournament trail has been as high as $5,000 a year, and following Demaret around the course is somewhat less difficult than trail-blazing for Gross.

I know only too well that there is a good deal of love's labor lost when I venture out for a round. The French have an expression for it, *C'est travailler pour le roi de Russe,* which means idiomatically "to work in the Russian salt mines." That is what caddying for Gross is like. Gross is aware.

Actually I had a real sharp caddy once. It was at the Pinecrest Lakes Country Club in Avon Park, Florida. I was playing with my friend Max Caplan, and our boy (carrying both bags of course) was reading the greens, clubbing us right, and even mumbling compliments after our less disastrous shots.

Then, coming up to the eighth green, our boy bent over and picked up a ten-dollar bill off the fairway. There was no one in sight. It was obviously his. Lost in a happy reverie he stumbled through a sand trap on to the green.

"Take the flag out," I suggested, naturally being away. Far away, as a matter of fact.

"Flag? Oh, yeah," he muttered.

"How will this green read?" I asked.

"I can't read this green."

"You were reading the others pretty well before you found that ten spot."

"The only kind of green I'm reading now is the kind I got in my pocket."

But must we suffer the slings and arrows of a caddy's flippancy along with our own inefficiency? Can't we have the caddies share moments with us when it is pleasant to smell the new-mown grass along the fairways, enjoy the sun, the scenery and a well hit shot? Demaret says yes and offers a story to prove it.

He knows a caddy named Skeets, who was Bob Hope's regular. Demaret met Skeets at the Rose Bowl game. Jimmy knew what he had to pay for his ticket on the fifty-yard line and there was the caddy sitting one row behind him, in the best seat in the house.

"How'd you come up with that seat?" Jimmy said.

"Hope gave it to me," Skeets replied, as though Demaret should have known the answer without the need for asking.

"I imagine Bob treats you pretty well," Jimmy said.

"Why shouldn't he," Skeets said. "He'd damn well better. I've been looping for him for ten years and he's never had a bad lie yet."

Hope clearly knows when he's well off. But others treat their "regular" caddies with similar generosity even though they may not need such extraordinary service. The year Wiffy Cox won at Pinehurst he tipped his caddy, a boy named "Snowball," $150. The following year, when Cox returned to Pinehurst to defend his championship, he asked for the same caddy again, but was told Snowball no longer was available.

"We don't know what happened to him. He just disappeared after you won last year," the caddy master explained.

Cox found out soon enough. Just as the tournament was about to begin, Snowball reappeared.

"You done ruined my life," he accused Cox.

"How did I do that?" Cox said. "I was kind to you. How can $150 ruin your life?"

"I got married with that money," Snowball explained, "and my wife made me quit this business and take a job."

I remember a caddy I had at the Canterbury Club in Cleveland, renowned for its hellish traps. I spent a good part of one afternoon ankle-deep in the sand and each time I blasted out I boasted of my feat. From one sandtrap I almost emulated Doug Ford, who had holed out of a trap at Augusta to win the Masters in 1957. My ball stopped a bare inch from the pin.

"That's one shot I know how to play," I exploded from the depth of the pit.

"You ought to," the caddy said. "You're in there enough to get the practice."

I will always recall the day I played the El Rio course in Tucson, Arizona. My shots were booming. Irons were crisp, putts had eyes for the hole. But even during rounds such as this one started out to be, a man should keep a modest and sensible tongue in his head, lest the caddy put him in his place. But what duffer has that kind of sense?

One drive was a beautiful thing of power and direction. "A nice three-wood shot and a putt and I've got me a bird," I bragged to the caddy.

In my haste and overconfidence I looked up as I came down out of my backswing. The wood shot dribbled along the turf. As I stood there watching its pathetic journey, the caddy carelessly swung the putter in my direction.

"That's a man-sized putt you left for yourself, Mister," he murmured.

Why should I abide a witness to my travail whom I must placate and then pay?

For years I've listened to my caddies' remarks and allowed them to go unanswered, but recently there appeared a marvelous expression of my plight in *Sports Illustrated,* fittingly in a section called "Events and Discoveries." It was a four-line poem and in its simplicity lies the solution to 400 years of embarrassment wrought upon golfers by caddies. It was composed by Mal Mallette, who once pitched for the Dodgers, and, in light of his years in Ebbets Field in Brooklyn, shouldn't concern himself about the reactions of spectators:

> "I'd rather have a caddie cart
> Than a caddie live;
> Don't care for any witnesses
> To count the strokes that I've."

NINE

○ ○ ○ ○ ○ ○ ○ ○ ○ ○

Susan Anthony's revenge

IN MY OPINION it's nonsense for the experts to say that Babe Didrickson, Betsy Rawls, Barbara Romack, Betty Jameson and the Bauer sisters attracted the women to the links by proving they could beat the men at their own game. What attracted the women into golf in such alarming and household-disrupting numbers within recent years is the same thing that always attracted the dolls —the guys.

You've got no more chance of chasing the female back home to the *Kinder, Kirche* and *Kueche* than you have of curing a male who has been bitten by the golf bug. The female is not only more deadly, but more determined. I have it on the authority of a relatively recent indoctrinee who, through clenched teeth and decked out in the latest and most expensive fashions that a pro shop can supply, said: "I'm going to beat my husband at his own game if it kills me."

This competitive matron presently is taking five lessons a week at four bucks per half hour. She has chewed up the lovely lawn of her back yard with her clubs, has dropped her regular attendance at meetings ranging from the Aster

Growing Society to the Zenith Club, and has become the best customer the delicatessen in her town ever had.

I offer her case in evidence that the golfing widow of yesterday has become today's deepest divot digger. And we complaining men have nobody to blame but ourselves. The women couldn't keep us men home, so they joined us. It brings to mind the story of the gent who went out every night to spend his time and dough crawling from pub to pub while his wife stayed home caring for the kids, the cooking, and the lamp which burned in the window.

One night our friend came home only a bit the worse for his stops at various watering holes and found the wife nowhere in evidence. He went down to the corner bar and there was his wife just ordering a double shot of bourbon neat. He waited while she lifted the glass, downed it and began to choke on its fiery contents.

"My God," she said, spying her spouse after drying her tears and checking her cough. "This is terrible. How do you drink this stuff?"

"All these years," he answered, "you think I've been enjoying it. All this time you've been saying I'm out drinking and having fun. What do you say now?"

Now the women know, too, the indignities one undergoes on a golf course, but they won't admit it, not even when dribbling the ball from tee to green. They realize that they have grabbed yet another freedom and they're making the most of it. Susan B. Anthony was responsible for only the first step in female emancipation, but suffrage, cigarettes and bobbed hair were timid steps forward compared to the bold way women have taken over on golf courses. As Carrie Nation wielded an ax, so her descendants are wielding clubs.

"Every day out here is Ladies' Day," one pro commented. He insisted upon being anonymous, and who can blame him. The women monopolize his time taking lessons. The pro shop, formerly a male sanctuary, is packed with chattering females. The women, of course, ready with the slightest excuse to buy the latest fashions, sign poppa's name to the tab.

Jack Benny once said, "Give me my golf clubs, the fresh air and a beautiful partner, and you can keep my golf clubs and the fresh air." We may as well relax and enjoy it. The girl golfers are here to stay.

Some of them are not bad either. If you insist upon being completely honest, a few of them are even good. The majority, however, think that a tee is something to drink and cluck over. On the green they primp and pose like peacocks. When they are egged on from the rear by impatient and frustrated males, they assume airs of hurt innocence. On Sundays, when the male members descend on the course, en masse, some clubs must take precautions against traffic jams. They post new rules. "Ladies are prohibited from teeing off before 1 P.M." Thus, males are in effect warned: "Be late and you deserve what you get."

To put it mildly, it can be somewhat distasteful if the missus, just taking up the game, insists upon playing with her old man, thus lousing up a foursome which has had a standing Sunday morning date for five years. If that isn't bad enough, some men have even been put into that unpalatable position of having to teach their wives how to play.

Recently, I saw a friend giving his wife a lesson on the driving range. As he spotted me approaching him, he turned beet red. I could see that he was deeply embarrassed. He teaches diction in our town high school, but when he introduced me to his wife, he stammered as if he had a palsy of the vocal cords. Obviously his wife cared little about golf. All she wanted was a sense of togetherness, and after harassing her husband for years he finally had to give in. He would try, he promised, to teach her the fundamentals of the golf swing.

The woman was considerably overendowed physically, especially in the southern regions. When she found it was a trifle difficult to hit the ball properly she began to pout.

"Why can't I hit the ball, dear?" she asked her anguished husband.

"You're standing in your own way," he said truthfully, "and there's no way on earth I can make it easier for you to swing around yourself."

Embarrassed and angry, the wife lunged at the ball and swung with renewed determination. She was a little too close to poppa, however, and the clubhead cracked on his elbow with the satisfying sound of a 250-yard drive off the tee. The bone broke and never healed properly. The guy was left with a stiff left arm and, like former Open champ Ed Furgol, he went on from that point to become the club champion. Apparently the stiff elbow gives him control. He's won a mantelful of trophies and when guests are over he points them out proudly.

"The missus made me what I am today," he tells his guests.

There is a moral here, but I haven't quite figured it out. The fact is, I haven't been able to solve much about the game of golf as it relates to women. For instance, how is it that a slight, delicate little china doll, who is too weak to do housework and needs a cleaning woman and a laundress, can play eighteen holes on a broiling summer day and never once complain that her feet hurt? Why is it that some of these dainty things who often manage to hit the ball up the middle and have such a fine touch on the greens have ten thumbs and two left feet once they are home again and pretending to be housewives?

Pretending, did I say? They're long past that stage. No sooner are the kids hustled off to school on crusts of stale bread and sour milk for breakfast than our one-time golfing widows scoot off to the club. By the time they get home

93

it's too late to cook a real meal. It's cold cuts and beans, a TV dinner, or "let's all go down to the delicatessen for a change."

For a change?

Bridge, Mah Jongg, gin rummy, and the ouija board were notorious enough for keeping a wife away from home. Now that she has found golf, however, she is out on the course all day, carries her troubles to the pro at the driving range at night, takes adult-education courses in swinging a golf club during the winter evenings, tosses out the kids' electric trains to set up a portable driving net in the basement, and picks her teeth with tees. It seems to me she's overdoing it.

Bill Roeder of the New York *World-Telegram and Sun,* who is something of a brassie buff, once asked Judy Frank, three-time metropolitan women's champion, why she quit tournament golf after becoming Judy Frank Jablow. Her explanation for her defection from the ranks should serve as a warning to those extremists of her sisterhood.

Judy said she knew of a prominent woman golfer whose husband had a big business deal cooking in Europe, which could make him wealthy for the rest of his days. Jubilantly he told his wife about the pleasant prospect and then, with great expectations, told her that he planned to make a second honeymoon out of the trip. They'd go over on a luxury liner leisurely and enjoy themselves.

"Absolutely not," said the golfing wife.

"But why?" her husband asked. "This is a wonderful opportunity for both of us."

"That just goes to show how little you think of me," the wife said. "Just when my swing's grooved, and I've got that certain feeling with my short irons, and my putts are dropping, you suggest a week aboard ship! I'd lose all of it! Do you really think I'd take that chance?"

"But honey, what's golf . . ." the husband started to say

94

when he saw the adamant look on his wife's face harden into concrete.

Then the solution struck him. "Tell you what," he said. "Suppose you can practice aboard ship?"

"That might work out," she said, "but I've got to have enough balls to practice every day."

"He got her five thousand brand new Titleists," Judy said, "and before the ship reached Europe she had hit every one of them into the ocean."

"That, brother, is love," commented Roeder. I assume he meant his love for her and hers for the game.

Most of early women golfers had leathery, seamy faces, knobby knees, muscles on their arms and varicose veins on their legs. Few of them bothered with the niceties of feminine dress, nor would it have helped. The male golfers ignored them. To paraphrase Dorothy Parker, men never chased a gal at all who ever cared to chase a ball. You couldn't have found a lipstick in the corner of the ladies' room. Their hair looked like ungroomed heather and they walked with the determined, rolling gait of cowhands.

How times have changed! A handicap committee woman told me about a conversation she had with a new member, with whom she was paired the first time.

"What's your handicap?" the new member was asked.

"With or without?" she asked.

"With or without what?"

"My girdle, of course," the new gal answered. "I'm nineteen when I don't wear it and twenty-four when I do."

Another time I waited on the tee while a foursome of gals, all shaped well enough to attract a second glance, were going off. The first three hit the ball fairly well. The fourth dug a divot behind it and trickled the ball up the fairway.

"I knew it. I knew it," she exploded.

"You knew what?" one of the others asked curiously.

"I knew I shouldn't have worn these shoes when I went out to play."

Two guys standing beside me guffawed. My urge was to do the same, but since I'd invented a few strange alibis in my time for my failure to get off a first tee, my sympathy stifled the giggle in my throat. The other women were not as compassionate.

"Don't tell me," one of them said, "that you must wear a special pair of shoes to hit the ball properly."

"Don't be silly," the embarrassed damsel replied. "I took all my lessons wearing high heels and now in these flat shoes this course is too high for me."

I've nothing against lipstick and a peek at oneself in the mirror occasionally. I can understand that a girl would want to look her cosmetic best coming into the clubhouse after the eighteenth hole. But a green isn't a ladies' room and no amount of my pleading, cajoling and threatening seems to hurry them along to the next tee. The truth is, I'd be happy if they didn't always wait to replenish their make-up after holing out on the short holes when there is another foursome waiting to hit up.

The fourteenth hole, a 103-yard par-three, at the Engineers Club is sneaky enough to drive a man to drink, and frequently does. The hole can be played with a wedge or a half 9-iron over a ravine. The green is a billiard table, but all about it there are more dangers than Dante himself could have devised. Old-timers at the club regale newcomers with the hoary bit that this was the hole on which Bobby Jones once took a nine.

At this hole I once demanded the right to play through a set of girls who were just gabbing away over hill and down dale. One of them had just holed out from about thirty feet, clapped her hands, squealed in delight and rushed up to hug and kiss her partner.

"That gives me an eleven," she stated proudly.

"Do you mind if I play through?" I asked.

96

"We're not holding you up, are we?"

"I do want to get through a little early. I have an appointment," I answered, chickening out slightly on a stronger statement I'd prepared in my mind.

They allowed me to precede them to the next tee, meanwhile chattering away like a covey of demented magpies. I glared as I teed up the ball. They ignored me. I glared again. So far as they were concerned, I didn't exist. I was determined to show them how a man gets the hell off the tee with dispatch, efficiency and power. I shanked my drive, which landed with uncanny accuracy on the tee from which I had just come.

"Excuse me," one of the angels cooed sweetly. "Didn't you just play that hole?"

I once knew a very attractive female golfer so desperate for a game that in a weak moment she went out for a round with the clubhouse wolf. The lady shanked an iron into virtually impregnable rough, and Wolfie went in with her to help locate her ball. It was found under a low-hanging tree deeply surrounded by thorn bushes, with barely room for a person to wriggle in and take a whack at it. The lady, however, studied her predicament carefully, and as she did Wolfie made his move. He pretended to reach for the ball but stumbled and embraced her instead.

She shoved him off and said: "It should be apparent, even to you, that I am an unplayable lie."

Golf can make a jerk out of a man, but there is a point beyond which even jerks do not go. Come to think of it, somebody once analyzed the golf swing as a series of inconsequential jerks which, when put together, makes a minor jerk feel like a monumental jerk.

There is a certain indefinable subtlety about this game and all hazards appertaining thereto, including the women who have overrun golf courses as though they were bargain basements on sales days. If you're patient, however, willing to swallow your dignity, and able to wait for the proper time to strike back, there is always the chance for the moment of vengeance. It may be fleeting when it comes, but it is sweet. A neighbor was telling me with almost psychotic pleasure about such a moment of truth in his lifetime of torment.

He loved the game, despite his frustrations on the course and his wife's incessant nagging that he devote more of his time to her. For years his week-ends at the club were his pleasure and his therapy which did more for him than could any psychiatrist's couch.

But the missus finally decided she had been a golfing widow long enough. One Sunday morning she surprised him when he awakened to take off for the course. There she was all smiles, an iron in her hand, a canvas bag on her back, and done up like Mrs. Sandy McNiblick.

"I've decided to play with you today, dear," she said. "We'll grab a cup of coffee at the diner and have a fine time on the links."

"What are you talking about?" the husband sputtered. "I've *got* a game. Besides, you never held a golf club in your hand before, except to beat the carpets."

"That's how much you know," she said. "For the last month I've been taking lessons. Isn't that a wonderful surprise?"

A man mugged at night in a dark alley couldn't have been any more shocked, but no amount of argument could get hubby out of this neat little *cul de sac* into which his missus had finessed him. All the way to the course he seethed inwardly. As he and his wife waited at the tee to get off, you could almost hear his teeth grinding in exasperation. He barely mumbled a hello to the three men with whom he regularly played. They sized up the situation quickly and knew enough to turn the other way. A golfer recognizes the danger signs in such situations. If nothing else, the game increases his knowledge of marital psychology.

98

Poppa was so angry by the time his turn came to tee off that he tried to take his rage out on the ball. He pushed his shot into the woods and started to stalk off after it.

"Wait for me," momma called. "I haven't stroked yet."

One stroke in the family would be enough, and poppa looked as though he were about to have it. But people were watching. He motioned his wife to the ladies' tee, where she managed somehow to get her club in contact with the ball. It trickled along the fairway and she was ecstatic. "I hit it! I hit it!" she gleefully cried.

Poppa didn't do much better for the next four holes. The fifth borders a recently built housing development. In one back yard the homeowners were enjoying their Sunday leisure, newspaper and coffee cups in disarray on the lawn, when suddenly the peaceful scene was shattered when poppa shanked an iron shot over the fence and between the chairs on which this gent and his wife were sitting.

The woman screamed and spilled her coffee. The man jumped to his feet shouting through the chain fence which separated their property from the course.

"You stupid idiot!" he shouted. "You almost hit my wife with that damned ball."

Our berserk friend flung his iron over the fence.

"There," he yelled. "Get even. Take a shot at mine."

It occasionally happens that the woman of the house learns to play the game better than the man, and when this occurs a man's home is transformed from his castle into his padded cell. His wife patronizes him with tips on how to improve his game, offers to watch him hit a few buckets at a practice range. The guy's just got to quit the game eventually on the pretext that business has become too demanding for him to waste his valuable time on a silly sport.

At first glance this may seem cowardly, but it really isn't. There is nothing more debilitating to one golfer than to have a better one constantly regaling him with the beauti-

ful recovery he made on the eleventh. When it's the missus, the end has come. A husband can stand his wife's nagging far more easily than he can her bragging.

There is one incident which puts the grisly business of women golfers into its proper perspective for me. It concerns a woman who consistently beat her husband at the game. One day after being thoroughly whipped, the husband stalked off the course and wasn't seen again for weeks. The wife continued to play every day, but this time with the other girls.

One Tuesday she begged off her regular game, explaining that she had a date to play with her husband again.

One of the girls watched from the dining room as the man teed off and later said to the wife, "Your husband is hitting the ball better now that he has a new stance."

"That," said the golfing wife, "isn't a new stance. It's a new husband."

TEN

○ ○ ○ ○ ○ ○ ○ ○ ○ ○

Links and liars

FEARLESS OSCAR FRALEY of United Press International once interviewed Joe Dey, executive secretary of the United States Golf Association, and came away with a startling bit of mathematics and morals.

Said Fraley, quoting Dey, "No more than two per cent of the players know and abide by the rules." Said Fraley, interpreting: "At least ninety-eight per cent who play golf are cheats."

When Dey read his words in print, he backtracked and extracted a post-mortem from Fearless Fraley. "You wouldn't even find one per cent who *actually* cheat."

Of course, if you're playing with an opponent who has a low handicap, such as 20-20 vision, you may not be inclined to cheat. You may try, but you're likely to be caught. You might even find yourself ostracized in the clubhouse for having been apprehended, but it's a peculiar thing how winter lasts deep into July, August and September when you come up with a bad lie and decide to give yourself a better one under winter rules.

All the practices employed in hustlers' rackets—shell games, Brooklyn Bridge auction, gold-brick, bargain-basement sales, and ocean-liner poker—look like inching at marbles compared to what goes on on the green grass under the bright blue sky. Surely, the practitioners here are more devious and the suckers more gullible.

To be strictly rule-abiding, for example, a golfer should be as careful as a surgeon in the operating room. From tee to green a ball must not be touched by human hands. Most golfers, however, who wouldn't think of short-changing a blind newsdealer, will hoodwink their opponents at every opportunity. They'll pick up the ball after every whack, wipe it, caress it, and proceed to give themselves a better lie.

Many golfers who spend hours cultivating patches of grass at home become more devastating than a swarm of locusts once they descend on a course. Vegetation is recognized in the rule book as a natural hazard, but ride on a Sunday along any road paralleling a golf course and you will see golfers on their hands and knees tearing up the countryside. They'll yank out handfuls of grass, tufts of weeds, clumps of gorse, and trample bushes, shrubs and seedlings in order to make a shot easier. The regulation that a ball must be played where it lies is observed as loosely as an international treaty.

I knew a man who carried a saw strapped to the side of his bag. Each time he found himself below the branches of a tree which obstructed his backswing, he'd whip the saw from the bag, remove the offending limb and blithely explain, "That was a dead branch. I'm allowed to remove it as an obstruction."

A variation on this innocent bit of knavery occurs each time a golfer approaches a water hole. Immediately he'll call to the caddy to look into the side pocket of the bag for an old ball he doesn't mind losing in the drink. Once across the hazard he'll substitute a new ball without the slightest twinge of conscience, although he is aware he has broken a rule.

Then there's the sand-trap ploy. Beware the golfer who

103

approaches his ball in a trap talking casually about Khrushchev, Zsa Zsa Gabor, and the Yankee slump. He thinks you can only see him from the waist up. If you creep on hands and knees to the edge of the green and peer down into the trap, you'll see him digging a trench beneath his ball with his wedge. That's called improving the lie, and this liar is an expert at it from way back.

Honesty may be the best policy, but on the golf course it is a rare thing. As Monsieur Jacques Henri François Villon, the French expert de links, once said: *Honi soit qui mal y pense.* Very roughly translated, this means, "Set a thief to catch a thief," and what better place than the golf course, where bankers who deal blithely in millions can't count six strokes from tee to green.

There is a renowned dancer who has an excellent reputation as a golfer, but his footwork on the stage can't possibly equal it in the rough as he toes his ball into a more playable position. There is also a pitcher for a big league team who has better control with his hand mashie than he has with his curve. I know a clothing manufacturer who supplied his regular caddy with a special pair of trousers. It had extralarge back pockets to carry balls and a slash for side pockets on each leg, but they were false pockets. When his patron needed a quick helping hand and a better position, the caddy surreptitiously put his hand into one of the fake pockets, and dropped a ball down his trouser leg.

Anybody with the proper gall can beat the rules, but it requires a certain type of genius to delude *yourself* into a lower score. It requires "chutzpeh," which is a word that defies definition. The stranger I encountered at the Oakwood Golf and Country Club in Kansas City had it. This one bragged about how well he played and took umbrage when I refused to allow him to concede himself putts longer than three feet.

"But I know I can sink that putt," he said. "Why must I prove it to you?" With that he picked up his ball instead of trying to knock it into the cup from four feet out and unashamedly proclaimed, "That gives me a par." And he believed it.

He was like the man who shot his ma and pa and then appeared before the court and asked for clemency on the grounds he was an orphan. That's chutzpeh.

When you play with a character like this you might as well allow him to keep the scorecard. You don't ask him his score and believe it; you know he's already discounted it. I knew a man who would mark his ball on the green after every putt and move it closer to the cup each time. I stood it as long as my tongue would allow. After two markings on the seventh hole, I suggested he pick up the ball. "If you mark it once more there won't be any ground to putt it out."

Satire doesn't touch them, nor wit, nor even direct accusation, because golf has a strange effect upon such people. It provides them with a hard thick shell of callousness on the outside. A golfer caught in a flagrant attempt to steal a stroke brazens out his larcenous tendencies with far more *savoir-faire* than he would if accused of being unfaithful to his wife or dishonest in his business dealings.

There would appear to be a deep sense of accomplishment and satisfaction that comes from getting away with a four when you might have had a five or perhaps a six. Otherwise there wouldn't be so many whiffies described as practice swings and so many strokes declared to be echoes.

There is the hoary tale told many times and repeated here only because it happens to be true and sooner or later it happens to you or somebody you know. It happened to my neighbor Al White, who was playing with an opponent who shall remain nameless because the code of the course is much the same as the code of the underworld, and what do you think I am, a stoolie?

Al allowed Mr. Anonymous to be the day's bookkeeper, although, being well acquainted with the gentleman's reputation, he kept a close mental tally on how many strokes his opponent took from tee to green. After both had holed out the first, the opponent asked Al: "What did you have?"

"Five," Al answered.

"I had a four," the other said.

At the completion of the second hole, the opponent politely inquired: "Your score, please?"

"Make it five again," Al replied.

"I had another four," his opponent said.

After both had holed out on the third green Mr. Anonymous put the question again to Al.

"Uh, uh," said Al. "It's my turn to ask first."

Golf is not only physical calisthenics and mental gymnastics, but also an immoral exercise which operates on the *caveat emptor* principle. It is a purgative, which enables a player to rid himself of all his baser inclinations, after which he can return to the world of normalcy cleansed as a lamb.

Long ago golf stopped being a gentleman's game, peopled only by the polite, considerate and proper. There is more con than conscience, more cussing, cussedness, chicanery and conspiracy on a golf course than you'll find in a poolroom on skid row.

We can write off the professional scroungers and scavengers who make their living at the game on certain Florida and California courses hustling marks like card sharps. This is hustling on a professional scale. If a golfer lets himself get inveigled by "the Fat Man" at Miami's Normandy Shores, he deserves to be taken. In the Calcutta scandal at Deepdale on Long Island or the manipulations that go on at LaGorce in Florida, there should be little sympathy wasted on the victims. They knew, or should have known. And any golfer who bucks sharp practices he knows exist rates being exposed to poverty and penury because he couldn't resist sticking his putter where it didn't belong. The concern here, however, is with our friends, neighbors and locker mates, who would accept three buttons in change from the church plate, but lose their balance completely at the prospect of winning a shiny golf ball through shady practice.

I was told about a fellow who showed up at the Indianapolis Speedway golf course just before the last 500-mile auto race. He borrowed clubs from the pro shop and then asked if it were possible to get a game. Another stranger was standing by and they were introduced.

"How well do you play?" the first asked the second.

"I'm just a hacker. Go around about a hundred, sometimes ninety-eight, sometimes ninety-five."

"That's fine," the newcomer answered. "I'm about the same, so let's play dollar Nassau to make it interesting."

Some three hours later the stranger returned the clubs he had borrowed, but not gratefully or graciously. He dropped the bag with a bang.

"Weren't the clubs any good?" the pro-shop attendant asked.

"What's the clubs got to do with it?" he groused. "You've got a helluva outfit here. You know that cheating s.o.b. I went out with? I had to shoot an eighty-four to beat him."

Country club golfers lie awake at nights contriving schemes which would have made the infamous swindler, Ponzi, look like an altar boy. There is even a case on record in which a golfer sued his club in court to raise his handicap. Many golfers falsify their own game and scorecards to obtain an advantage in tournaments, and the suspicion exists that many a man fooling around the scorecard rack is only waiting for the chance to forge an opponent's figures and lower his handicap.

Suspects are numerous and diverse at every club, only in golf it's a breach of etiquette to spotlight them. In any other sport they'd be cashiered, have their epaulets stripped, and be drummed out of the regiment, but in a game in which a sphere 1.68 inches in diameter is resting on another sphere 24,874 miles in circumference and must be knocked into a target 4¼ inches wide, it is considered perfectly normal for arithmetic to go awry. A golfer is many things, but he is not Univac.

Consider the case of a colleague of mine who wasn't even surreptitious in his unique scoring methods. He flaunted his chiseling in the faces of the other members of his foursome, but they didn't do much about it except grouse privately because they knew in their own hearts they were doing at least a little of their own.

One day, however, our finagler of the fairways was outdoing himself. He sliced one out of bounds off the first tee and set another ball down for a mulligan without so much as asking "By your leave." He dribbled the second one into a trap at the left and mumbled something about just experimenting. The third one managed to get off the ground and stay on the fairway.

"That's the way to start a round," he said.

"Start? What about the first two shots?" he was asked.

"What first two shots?" he said. "What's the matter with you guys? Got no heart or something? Didn't you see that dog run across the fairway? Want me to kill it or something?"

Maybe it was the surprising effect of having been called at last, but the gent played relatively honest pool for the next two holes and it proved just too much for him. His game went completely to pieces and he followed suit. He began to complain he wasn't feeling well. The others ignored him, having told a few imaginative alibis in their own time, but suddenly he began to sweat, said he felt dizzy and dropped to the ground, quivering.

"What's the matter with Joe?" one man said.

"I think he's having a stroke, Mister," said the scared caddy.

"Don't worry," said another, "he'll think of an excuse for not putting it on his scorecard."

There is little point in asking a man, "What is your score?" He can tell you what numbers have been inscribed on the card, but they don't necessarily reflect the truth. The scorecard might even be attested, notarized and stamped with the great seal of the U.S.G.A., but there is no enforcement agency—praise the lord—to guarantee accuracy.

Many an uncomfortable afternoon has been caused by somebody so obsessed with bookkeeping he gapes at you with a look of incredulous disgust after you announce what you did on the hole. He doesn't say he doesn't believe you. He merely stages a theatrical pause for a minute or more, doubt covering him like a poncho, and then turns in the direction from which both of you came. He begins calculating on his fingers, stabbing all the while to the spots from which you took each swing.

Worse, still, after clearly tallying off at least one stroke more than the number to which you've confessed, he says acidly, "Your honor."

There once was a scene in an old Mae West play in which she flashed a handful of diamonds at a girl friend, who said, "My goodness, look at those rocks." To which Miss West replied, "Goodness had nothing to do with it, dearie."

It is my fear that honor has little to do with it either and that most of those who pull the holier-than-thou routine on the golf course are hypocritical and sanctimonious and just lucky nobody's called them on *their* mathematics. To play a poor game and have high morals would be catastrophic. To play a good game is to have low morals. How else do you get to play that well, unless it is by neglecting business, home and family?

You see, I've looked into the direct scientific relationship between golfing and cheating. I've allowed myself to undergo a lie-detector test, deliberately telling whoppers

110

which would make Munchausen blush. By a coincidence which may not be strange my innards jumped about at the moment of telling the fibs just as they do every time I approach a course and all the time I'm on it.

It was explained to me that emotions are aroused when you lie, with the heart pumping extra blood and certain glands secreting juices, the effect of which is to start the needle to vibrating. Hence nobody should be surprised that Diogenes took one look at a roomful of golfers and fled in horror at the impossibility of his task.

It just happens that there is a natural affinity between links and liars that goes beyond alliteration. A golfer must have gall and he must have guile, and if he speaks with a forked tongue it is only because the devil intended it that way. But the oddest (yet most human) part of it all is that there is a kind of self-mesmerism in the fabrications. Listen to some of the locker-room liars tell some of their fantastic stories, and in no time at all you realize they're believing what they're saying. It's a kind of defense mechanism, a protective distortion which makes one man equal to the other.

If we abided by golf's demanding and spartan rules without deviation, we would become a nation of complex-ridden, harassed, uncertain saints whose scores would mount astronomically. We would be insulting and questioning each other on the course constantly, eventually making it impossible to get up a foursome whose members were able to stand each other. Instead perhaps it is the better part of wisdom that we shrug our shoulders understandingly and agree that this is in the nature of the game. And in the nature of the man.

It's an impossible game, even for those who make a living in it. Long-ball-hitting George Bayer once seven-putted a green at Oklahoma City and stalked out of the tournament. Maybe if so many people weren't keeping tabs on the

111

number of times he jabbed at the ball, this horrible memory wouldn't have to haunt Bayer wherever he goes the rest of his life.

I like my way better. It leaves me with a more placid disposition. I learned about it at Winged Foot, a month before the National Open, when the famed course was put on display for the press. The fairways had been narrowed by allowing the grass to grow along its sides. Not unexpectedly, my drive didn't fall where the grass had been cut.

"Let me have my three wood," I told the caddy.

Obediently he pulled it from the bag, but the look on his face was ample warning it wasn't the club to get under the ball in that kind of lie.

"Wrong club?" I asked.

"I'm only carrying the bag," he said, "but if you asked me to club you I wouldn't have picked that one."

All the while he was speaking, I had been tapping the flat of the club directly behind the ball, beating down the grass. The caddy watched the lie being bettered as the grass was lowered and the ball raised as though it were sitting on a tee.

"Well," I said, "if not the three wood, which one?"

"Just keep that up for a little while longer," the caddy answered, "and it'll be the perfect lie for the club you're holding."

I've even heard tell of the clergyman golfer who did a little cheating. That is, he was cheating to be out on the course at all. He should have been busily preparing his Sunday sermon, but the sun was out, the birds were chirping, and this man of cloth felt that old itchiness in his feet. He stole away to the course to play a quick nine all by himself—no caddy, no partner, no witnesses. Except for one. His Boss Upstairs observed this clandestine transgression and decided to mend the ways of this erring soul.

On the next hole the clergyman hit the perfect shot off the tee and it plunked into the cup. Up above, the Bossman nodded in satisfaction. A confused assistant standing by said, "Excuse me, Sir. But is this the way to fix a transgressor?"

"Do you know a better way?" asked the Boss. "For the first time in his life he's had a hole in one and he can't tell anyone about it."

ELEVEN

○ ○ ○ ○ ○ ○ ○ ○ ○ ○

You meet such interesting people

"WELL, ANYWAY, it's a beautiful day," is
the usual soporific with which the hacker consoles himself.
But this wasn't a beautiful day, at least not outside. It was
heavy and murky, with the threat of rain in the air, but
inside the birds were singing and my heart was light.

For once, my drives were cannon shots off the tee. My
fairway shots had eyes for the green. My putts seemed
magnetized for the cup. Norbeck Country Club in Washington, D.C., had never looked so lovely. For seven holes I
was one over par. I didn't believe it. I didn't want to think
about it. I wanted to stay automatic. I soaked in the admiring glances by Duke Zeibert, the Washington restaurateur
and golfing promoter, with whom I was playing.

When I deuced a par-three it was more than Zeibert
could bear. "I've never seen you play so well," he said.
"I've been trying to figure out why. I think I've got it.
You're whipping your hands into the ball. You should
keep thinking about that."

Who was thinking? I'd been in a groove and when you're
in a groove you don't have to think. Zeibert's remarks, however, pricked my consciousness. I started to think about

115

my hands. "Keep whipping them into the ball." The thought soon plagued me. That was all I needed. The reversion took place soon after. Jekyll changed back into Hyde. Mourning became Electra. Gross became himself, which is to say, "Duffer, where have you been?"

I'm not charging Zeibert with any insidious intent, but psychological warfare was conducted on the golf course long before the juice was slipped into Claudius' ear and Franco founded the fifth column. As a matter of simple psychosomatic fact, golfers have tried to rattle one another ever since the first Scot told the second that his kilt was flapping in the wind. It is a natural consequence of a game which requires absolute concentration. Your opponent will do his devious damndest to destroy your Yogalike absorption with the little ball.

One well-planted seed of doubt can grow into an oak tree of despair. One accurately aimed needle can do more than a broad sword in cutting down an opponent. If you want to be crude about it, you can sneeze, burp, cough, talk out loud while a man's addressing his ball, be sickeningly sympathetic about each blown shot, and then stand by to wait while your opponent blows his top. You can dawdle, take a dozen practice swings, sweep imaginary worms off the green with your cap, whistle merry tunes, suggest an alteration in his stance, grip and club selection, or say knowingly, "I think I know what you're doing wrong but I don't want to add to your confusion by telling you. You're mixed up enough already."

Have you ever played with the character who considers himself the master of everybody else's game, but can't solve his own? Not being able to play well himself, he transfers his own frustrations to you by becoming a self-appointed instructor. It always happens at the most unfortunate times. Let him par a hole by sheer luck and his cloying sympathy at your own misadventures takes on the most repulsive kind of patronizing.

"Well, now, aren't you lifting your club off the ground

too quickly? You're trying to kill the ball. What are you mad at it for? It hasn't done anything to you. Stop hitting from the top. You're not finishing your shot. Don't you think you ought to keep your head down while you're swinging?"

There should be a law which would allow you to take firm, positive police action against the human hazards you meet on the course. And yet the one time I ever saw anybody threaten retribution the prospective victim was innocent of nothing more than sneezing at the wrong time.

This fellow who was scheduled to play with a partner in a club tournament tried to beg off at the last minute because he had a bad cold. His partner, frantic because it was too late to team up with someone else, pleaded with his sick friend to play, and finally the incipient pneumonia case reluctantly acceded.

The twosome played well for the first five holes, and were tied for the lead. Suddenly partner number two—the "persuader"—went completely berserk. Something, perhaps an earthworm a foot and a half below the surface wending its weary way home, had called loudly enough to its mate to distract him. Maybe it was a butterfly bursting out of its cocoon with a freedom-loving cry which pierced his ears. In any event he mangled one shot after another. Between holes six and eight, his clubs acquired enough flying time to fulfill the Civil Aeronautics Board's requirement for a pilot's license. He ground his teeth in fury. Where he stamped no grass ever grew again, and only the fearless or the foolish would have breathed loud enough to be heard.

Then he stepped to the ninth tee. On the side lines our poor fevered friend felt the dreadful itch of inevitability which precedes the sneeze ... "Ah ... ah ... ah ... *choo!*"

The man never struck at the ball. He turned toward the culprit with the wildest imaginable look in his eyes, his face contorted in fury, his driver held above his head like an ax.

"I'm about to prove," he shouted, "that the common cold

can be fatal. You and your snuffling and your sneezing have ruined my concentration—why didn't you stay in bed?"

A round of golf is supposed to be approached with a sense of happy anticipation. The pros tell us we must think positively: Never remember the bad days. Avoid dwelling on the flubbed shots. Practice building confidence that a misplaced shot never will be repeated.

One golfer who thinks positively is Billy McGovern, an assistant pro at Grossinger's. McGovern refuses to regard the frantic chase as a crusade.

"The game's so easy it gets boring," he said to me. "It's all a matter of approaching it the right way."

All right—let's try it. If you approach it the way most people do, you come through the front gate, park the car and walk to the clubhouse.

On the way there are a few interruptions. For one thing, as you park the car you see a friend in the lot going through the golf swing, but something's missing. He has no club in his hands and his eyes are closed as though trying to re-capture a memory.

"What's with you?" you say, knowing damn well what's with him, but being morbidly curious as to exactly how he will explain it.

"I know what I want to do," he says, "but I can't make my body do it."

You mutter something sympathetic, all the while moving off quickly because you're determined to protect your skein of positive thinking from other people's problems.

Barney, the clubhouse attendant, greets you. He looks dour. You realize this is Tuesday. The club's closed Monday to gather up the week-end's debris from the course. Monday is Barney's day off which he always spends at the race-track, blowing a full week's tips.

"A photo," Barney says. "Beaten by a photo."

"Ah yes, into each life some rain," you say, moving

rapidly away, "must fall. But not in mine, but not in mine."

A few of the fellows already have played a round. They look as though they'd just come from a wake.

"How'd you play?" you ask, not really caring, but being polite.

"Don't ask," one says, "I don't even want to think about it." But he can't think about anything else.

"If," he says, "I didn't push that shot into the trap on the first, and if I'd gotten a good kick on my second shot on the second, I wouldn't have blown up on the third. And why don't they fix that damned hill on the fourth?"

So there you are. In the time it takes to get out of your street clothes and into your playing clothes you've been as thoroughly draped in crepe as if you'd visited a mortuary. The locker room mourners have woven their depressing spell, and your own morbid imagination has begun to work overtime beforetime. The dirge already is ringing in your ears. You feel the knot hardening in your stomach. Your hands begin to sweat. Your positive thinking begins to evaporate even before you have a chance to address the ball.

This is the way it happens.

I sneak away from my office early one day to get in some badly needed practice at my club.

"There's a threesome ready to go off, Mr. Gross," the starter says. "Do you have a game or do you want to join them?"

The three are warming up on the tee. I have no game and I can wait, but that could ruin another hour and the wife hasn't been burning the candle in the window lately. She's just been burning.

"I'll join them if they'll have me," I say, and approach the threesome on the tee. One is hitting at an empty pack of cigarettes with a fury the executioner must have shown when he chopped off Anne Boleyn's head. Another is posed like a statue over the ball. The third has a rule book stuck

120

in his back pocket. At one time or another I've played with each of them, and I remember their idiosyncrasies with distaste.

That third fellow is a strange combination. He's the golf-course lawyer, who pulls the book on you any time it serves his advantage. He doesn't play eighteen holes; he plays eighteen Hoyles. He's also the comedian who'd violate the most fundamental rules of etiquette and decency because they're not to be found in the pages of his rule book. He's a rub-of-the-green man, but he rubs you the wrong way without even trying.

I remembered a round I played with him previously which points up the companionship he provides. On an early hole he grounded his wedge in the trap, but pretended not to know it. He was removing a few dead branches from beneath his ball when the ball moved. I gave him a warning look that should have shriveled his soul. He didn't blink an eye.

On the next hole one of our foursome landed in a deep bunker and had trouble getting out. The guy took two blasts, almost extricated himself, but the lip overhung and the ball rolled back into the trap. From deep within the trap he muttered imprecations at himself.

"If you dig that hole any deeper," said the comedian lawyer with a self-appreciative howl, "you'll have to join the excavators' union."

The furious man of the threesome I have been invited to join is a club thrower. He also has been known to slam a putter on the green when a putt goes awry, taking a divot out of it without the slightest trace of conscience. Once he wrapped a club around the water cooler, breaking the porcelain drinking spout. On another occasion, he stormed into the clubhouse and left an angry imprint the size and shape of his shoe on the locker-room door. The clubhouse attendant was tempted to slip him a mickey, but decided the man's acid disposition would nullify the drink's effect.

The last of the threesome is the least objectionable. He is studying to be a memory expert. He is a perfectly compatible companion except for one thing. He stands above the ball calling on his well-trained memory to reel off in infinite detail exactly what each arm, leg and muscle is about to do. He stands and stands and as I watch him my mind goes cloudy and, like Hamlet, I lose my resolution.

I describe this foursome because it is not an unusual one. Some days my luck is worse than this. On occasion I find myself paired with the gambler. He's the fellow who can't play a round without having so many bets it would require a totalizator to figure them. By the time they are reckoned the guy has insisted upon pressing the bets, and should he lose he isn't exactly hasty about paying off. This way you've got a series of pluses and minuses going all year with enough debits and credits to drive a C.P.A. to B.&B.

I might also wind up with the alibier, who has an excuse, no matter how tenuous, for every shot which doesn't find its way in a direct line to the hole. Occasionally, too, I have played with the ball hawk, who is probably the most low-down of members. He walks with a permanent stoop. You'll find his blood relative at the race tracks bending from the waist, his eyes cast on the ground looking for winning mutuel tickets which have been thrown away by mistake.

There he's known as a stooper. At golf clubs, where things are more genteel, he's known as a cheap s.o.b., especially by the pro, from whom he never buys balls. However, he's never out of balls, although he has yet to take a swing at a virgin. From tee to green this guy rarely walks on the fairway, except to cut across to take his shot. He tours the entire course bent over, his club swinging grass, scrub and weeds out of the way, his eyes glued to the ground for other people's balls lost in the rough and not recovered.

The caddies hate him. They consider him a poacher on their territory. But the ball hawk is oblivious of insult, wasted time, the burrs which stick to his pants.

When I play with the ball hawk he won't let me take too much time trying to recover my own ball which may have strayed. He wants me to take the penalty and drop a new one, but all the time he's like Captain Kidd marking a map for hidden treasure. The next time around he'll know where to look, and if my initials happen to be engraved on the ball he plays with the following week-end, I'll know he came back that way and made a splendid recovery. He operates on the theory that finders keepers, losers weepers, and I could cry my eyes out before this scavenger would admit M. G. might possibly mean Milton Gross.

It would be difficult to find that out, though, because the ball hawk selects his company carefully and matches the balls he plays with his companions of the moment. He hoards his supply of other people's balls in a padlocked box in his locker and sleeps with the key around his neck.

Once the boys decided to get square. They jimmied the lock and substituted a batch of trick balls with off-center balances.

Weeks went by before Ball Hawk, all unknowing, chose one to play with. On the first green he reached into his pocket to substitute a clean ball for the putt in place of the battered, bedraggled one with which he had come thus far.

When he tapped it with his putter the ball started for the cup, swerved right, swerved left, and then almost doubled back to where he was standing, or rather hopping about.

"Why, the cheap, chiseling, cheating louse!" the ball hawk exploded. "What a low down trick! What kind of cheap balls are they selling at the pro shop? Whoever did that would ring in shaved dice in a friendly crap game."

123

To me golf has become like war. It is a battle of attrition, and to borrow an old gag from Mac Davis' *Say It Ain't So,* there are times when I feel like a Civil War hero—out in 61, back in 65.

The lone consolation is that I have company, lots of it and it pleases me to realize that my occasional 96 gives me more real pleasure than the scratch golfer gets from his 80. I know a few of them who are in torment when they three-putt a green or bogey a hole.

These are golfers who no longer are fighting the battle to master their bodies. They are grooved, effortless swingers who do not have to indulge in memory exercises each time they step up to the ball. But even to these paragons something happens every so often to short-circuit the even flow of the message their minds send to their muscles.

I saw it happen to Slamming Sammy Snead, one of the sweetest swingers in the history of the game. He lost his touch completely for a few holes in the 1958 Masters. His accuracy gone, he took himself to the practice tee, where hour after hour he banged away at his iron shots.

Then, when it didn't count, Sammy regained his artistry. He shifted his caddy around as he shifted his clubs, and the boy shagging for Sammy became his target. It was worth the boy's life to take his eye off the ball when Snead hit it. The balls were bouncing at his feet or coming at his head as though Snead had zeroed in with a bomb sight.

Snead finally decided he'd had it. His touch had returned, and he called in his caddy as the day's work ended.

"Well," Snead said, anxious as any of us for commendation from a caddy. "How'd you like that?"

"Looks to me, Mr. Sam," said the caddy, "that you're nothing but a practice player."

In quarters I inhabit such a remark is an invitation for a duel with 5 irons, but so often it happens to be the plain, simple, unvarnished, painful truth, because golf is more mental than physical.

125

The idea of the game is to put the ball into the hole and nobody stops you but yourself, although sometimes it does seem they have covers over the cup. When you believe you can do it, half the battle is won. The crime of our time is that there are so many unbelievers.

TWELVE

o o o o o o o o o

Temper, temper

I HAVE DONE considerable research on
the golfing phenomenon known as popping your cork—
also known as blowing your stack, flipping your lid, what's
happened to Vesuvius? and thar he blows. However, there
is more to research than the theoretical side, as Kinsey set
out to prove in another area.

As a case history, I refer to terrible tempered Tommy
Bolt, the 1958 Open champion, who has popped more
corks than the wine stewards at the Waldorf. Scarcely a
round goes by that Bolt doesn't fizz, effervesce and explode.
During the 1953 Tournament of Champions, nicknamed
"The Slot Machine Open" by columnist Joe Williams because of its Las Vegas location, certain gamblers demon-
strated a unique interest in Bolt.

Tommy was two under par at the tenth hole of the first
round. He yipped a 4-foot putt and broke his putter. Two
holes later his drive got a bad bounce and landed in the
rough. Bolt smashed his driver into pieces. Inasmuch as
the rules forbid a player in a tournament to replace broken
clubs, Tommy finished the round with twelve clubs, two

under regulation. He putted thereafter with his 2-iron and drove with the 2-wood.

The next day Wilbur Clark, the host at the Desert Inn, made book on Bolt, not whether he'd finish first in the tournament, but that he would finish the second round with fewer than the regulation fourteen clubs in his bag. The odds were 6-5 against Bolt, but surprisingly few of those Las Vegas experts on the volatility of human nature would bet that Bolt could contain himself sufficiently through eighteen holes of golf to keep his set of clubs intact. Tommy managed it, but only because the clubs proved durable. After Bolt had blown a chip shot, he bounced the iron to the ground, but the shaft didn't break. Clubs obviously are steeled better these days than the people who use them.

"It's perfectly normal for otherwise rational human beings to erupt so violently on the golf course," says a famous psychiatrist to whom I brought this singular problem. The psychiatrist also happens to be a golf addict. He communes with his clubs each week-end to escape from his patients and be able to face another five days of listening to their troubles. On the course he lets himself go, breaking and throwing clubs, cussing the caddies, storming off the green, and otherwise ridding himself of all his frustrations.

"When I miss a shot that I've made so many times before, I am beside myself with rage," he says. "Mr. Bolt doesn't get any more upset than I do about it. There is a sense of exhibitionism in all men as well as a sense of pride, and nowhere do these two come more in conflict than on the course. I find golf the finest safety valve for my own inner tensions. I'm just happy, though, that I do not have to make a living out of the game," concluded the psychiatrist.

Many people strike at the ball as though they anticipated it striking back. In one way or another it usually does, with

129

repercussions so devastating you'd think the player had stepped on a land mine. Golf courses are booby-trapped far more sadistically than any other playground.

"Golf," said Lloyd Mangrum to Mel Durslag, of the Los Angeles *Examiner,* "is the only sport I know in which a player pays for every mistake. In other words, a man can muff a serve in tennis, miss a strike in baseball or throw an incomplete pass in football and still have another chance to square himself. But in golf every swing counts against you. Competing under such strain, the golfer naturally gets mad."

"The sport," Bob Rosburg observed, "isn't like any other where a player can take out all that is eating him on an opponent. In golf it's strictly you against your clubs."

Accordingly, there have been some wild, weird and wonderful reactions when the ball does not go where the club directed it. Rosburg, himself, for instance, will not boil in public. He prefers privacy for his eruptions. In one tournament he missed a short putt, walked off the green and barged into a screen of thick shrubbery. Most observers guessed he had gone off to relieve himself. He had, indeed, but not in the way nature intended. Hidden from view he smashed his putter. The destruction done, he returned, purged and purified, to continue his game.

There was a pro in the 1930s named Lefty Stackhouse. Right off one has to be cautious of the gentleman because, like me, he played the game backward. When he missed shots he'd belt himself several accurately placed uppercuts to the chin. One day he really lost control. He placed his hand upon the ball washer and rapped on it with his putter until he broke several bones in his fingers. Though Stackhouse was obviously operating on the Biblical theory that one must pluck out an offending organ, some narrow-minded tournament officials took a jaundiced view of so vengeful an attitude. They considered rapping him with a two-stroke penalty for damaging club property.

Even President Eisenhower simmers in the summer heat when his game goes astray. According to Ed Dudley, former pro at Augusta National Golf Club, the President reacts violently within himself to his lapses into dufferdom.

"First," said Dudley, "he clams up. He won't say a word. Second, he doesn't walk to his ball. He runs to it. He can hardly wait to get even."

Perhaps that is the answer. There is a sense of vengeance in all of us, especially when that offending ball just sits there waiting to be whacked.

Peter Wilding played a course in Scarborough, England, and probably will remember the round for the rest of his limping life.

At one point Peter's ball landed in the rough, but instead of coming all the way out on his recovery shot, it hopped into the air and dropped into his trouser cuff. Peter was faced with an agonizing choice: either he stuck by the rules and played the ball where it lay, or he retrieved the ball from his cuff and lost a stroke. He chose the former way and thereby merited having a tablet cast—well, some kind of a cast, because that's what he wound up in.

With one painfully accurate swing, he chipped both the ball to the fairway and the bone in his ankle.

The conclusion which inevitably must be drawn is that nobody is immune to violent moments, whether he be the pro playing for thousands or the duffer playing for exercise. What gets exercised usually is your temper, no matter how placid a person you are.

Harold Weissman, the sports columnist of the New York *Daily Mirror,* once was as even-tempered a man as it was possible to encounter, but when he discovered golf he also discovered a hidden streak of violence within himself.

When we're on the course together it is just a question of who blows soonest. On one occasion the waiting must have been too much for both of us. We made a solemn vow we'd allow nothing to bother us. By the time we reached the ninth at Fenway in New York not a word of anger had been uttered aloud. But the hissing was ominous. Both of us had begun to turn purple and if pricked with a pin we'd have popped like balloons. For an hour and a half we had been cutting the heads off dandelions, screeching at caddies for having underclubbed or overclubbed us, and growling at each other.

By the thirteenth hole I'd had as much of Weissman as I could stand. By coincidence he felt the same way about me. By the sixteenth I was just waiting for him to turn his back. By the eighteenth I wouldn't have dared turn mine to him. As we paid off the caddies I said, "That's it. I'm through with this idiotic game. I'll never go out on a golf course again."

"I've been thinking the same thing," Harold said. "We've been friends for so many years we shouldn't allow this stupid game to break us up."

"We'd better cool off," I suggested. "I'm going down to the bar. Let's cool off with a drink."

"You go on down," Weissman said. "I'll meet you there. I want to talk to somebody here first."

We took our leave of each other. Instead of heading for the bar, however, I crossed over to the first tee. I wanted to test a thought which had suddenly come to me. I was certain it would correct my slice. The experimental ball took off like a shot. I hefted my bag and went after it. The green looked so inviting I pitched to it and the ball dropped dead with the flag.

A sunk putt, another drive off the second tee, and another shot toward the second green and I had completely forgotten my date with Harold. Almost two hours later, still carrying my own bag and following my balls where they landed, I was back at the ninth green.

"Damn!" the thought suddenly struck. "I didn't meet Harold at the bar. He'll never talk to me again now."

132

But there he was, meek as a lamb, dragging his own bag behind him, coming off the eighteenth.

"What happened to you?" we said simultaneously.

"I was coming down to meet you," he said, "but I suddenly got an idea how I could straighten out my hook. I decided to hit a ball off the tenth to see how it would work, and then I figured I might as well keep on as long as I was hitting so well."

"Do you think we ought to have that drink now?" I asked.

"To hell with the drink," Harold answered. "Let's go out for another nine."

I have it on good authority that no golfer, good or bad, ever has learned to control his temper completely. I have seen golfers pound their heads against trees, deliberately kick at their own legs with their spiked shoes, wade unmindfully into a creek to whack at a ball they couldn't remove with a dredge, much less a wedge, scold a caddy with profanity that would blanch a sailor's parrot, and then come off the course describing how relaxing a game golf is.

It's so relaxing that such as Ben Hogan go days without eating at tournament time, although outside he appears as calm as a poker-faced Indian. Jimmy Demaret, who is the most easygoing of men, played a practice round with Hogan on the Augusta National course a week before both were to play for the big money in the Masters. Augusta must be the most beautiful golf layout in the world. In the rough on each hole a different kind of flower is planted, and if golf were the kind of game to grow lyrical about, this would be the most delightful course to get into trouble. As Jimmy describes his own feelings about the course, "One hole looks and smells prettier than the last."

That may be Demaret's feeling, but it certainly wasn't Hogan's. On the eleventh, Jimmy belted one deep into the

133

rough. When he went in to find the ball, the beauty of the flowers and their scent made him feel magnificently alive.

"Ben," he said to Hogan, "don't you just love to get into the rough here?"

"I don't like to get into the rough *anywhere*," Hogan growled.

"I'm glad he stayed out of it," Jimmy concluded. "He would have bitten the tops right off those beautiful flowers."

Although pros have more riding on each stroke, you don't have to be a pro to blow your stack. As a matter of fact, most pros are more circumspect than amateurs. The pro is subject to fines and suspensions, the amateur only to his conscience—which is all that's left, though badly shattered and hardly recognizable, after he's eaten his heart out.

Inasmuch as a golfer will accept any ready alibi for his own shortcomings as quickly as an ostrich will seek a hole to bury its head, the volcanic eruptions could be charged to the stresses and strains of our hectic modern world. But this is nothing more than the feeblest excuse. In golf 'twas ever thus. Atomic fallout may have changed the weather and poisoned some fish, but it hasn't altered one whit or one bit the emotional climate in which the golfer functions. The more things change, the more they remain the same.

I happened upon a volume called *The New Golfer's Almanac for the Year 1910* in which are reprinted observations on golf, golfers' habits and inclinations. One of the monographs, by A. J. Balfour, M.P., is entitled: "Swearing," originally published in 1890 in the *Badminton Book on Golf*.

Now, we may have a few new words they didn't have then, but you will see how little has changed since this right honorable English duffer penned the following some seventy years ago:

"Expletives more or less vigorous directed against himself, the ball, the club, the wind, the bunker, and the game, are the most usual safety-valve for the fury of the disappointed golfer. But bad language is fortunately much gone out of use; and, in any case, the resources of profanity are not inexhaustible. Deeds, not words, are required in extreme cases to meet the exigencies of the situation; and, as justice, prudence, and politeness all conspire to shield his opponent from physical violence, it is on the club that under these circumstances vengeance most commonly descends. Most players content themselves with simply breaking the offending weapon against the ground.

"But some persons there are whose thirst for revenge cannot be satisfied by any such rapid or simple process. I have been told of one gentleman who threw the offending club on the ground, and then with his niblick proceeded to punish it with piecemeal destruction, breaking its shaft into small pieces very much as criminals used to be broken on the wheel. Even this procedure seemed inadequate to one infuriated golfer of whom I have heard.

"A shaft, be it broken into ever so many fragments, can be replaced and the implement be as good as new. Nothing less than destroying both head and shaft can insure its final disappearance from the world of Golf. The club must not merely be broken, but must be destroyed, and from its hated remnants no new race must be permitted to arise for the torment and discomfiture of succeeding generations of golfers.

"This perfect consummation can, it is said, be attained by holding the club upright, the head resting on the ground, then placing one foot upon it and kicking it with the other, just at the point where the head and shaft are bound together. By this simple expedient (which I respectfully commend to the attention of all short-tempered golfers) a 'root and branch' policy may be effectually carried out by destroying at one stroke both the essential parts of the club. It is better to smash your clubs than to lose your temper."

As is immediately evident, Mr. Balfour, Esq., got himself right down to the fine grain of the wood. However, we do have a slightly more complicated problem today. Steel shafts are far more difficult to demolish than hickory. Also the price of clubs is somewhat higher than it was in Balfour's day which poses to the irate golfer the question, must I blow my bankroll along with my cork?

THIRTEEN

o o o o o o o o o

Ducking the pro

I WAS CHOPPING my way around the course followed by a stolid, though thoroughly disgusted, caddy, who would offer neither advice nor solace. His job, he felt, was to carry my bag, extend the club I requested, keep his eyes open for strayed balls, and keep his mouth shut.

In desperation, finally I pleaded for help. "Tell me one thing," I whined, "just one thing that I'm doing wrong."

"You're ducking the pro," the caddy said.

Maybe it's just as well that some of us do. Otherwise the pros would wind up with all our pesos and very little patience. How much duffery can a pro take from the likes of me, hour after hour, day in day out? Will he teach me before I ruin him?

If you reduce the golf swing to its basic elements, it shouldn't really be so complex. There is a ball, a club and you slugging away in the wilderness. But there is also a good deal of professional gobbledegook which is guaranteed to destroy that simplicity.

For instance, how can a duffer know what a pro means when he says, "Let the clubhead do the work." Until the

clubhead does do the work he'll never understand the feel of it and once that happens it's entirely possible he may never recall it. "You must get your left side out of the way," another pro advises, and a third stresses the absolute need for getting the hands into the shot. Another tells you to hit against a firm left side, and still another insists you must do all your thinking before you address the ball so that by the time you're swinging there's not a thought in your head.

There is one pro whose theory on the golf swing is the most unique of all. Many start the novice with gags, gimmicks and gadgets, but this pro defines the golf swing in terms of a rope. He has a piece of clothesline to which he has attached a weight at the end. The golf swing, he says, is much like the pull of the weight against the rope as centrifugal force is brought into operation.

Mark Sherwin, news editor of the *New York Post,* is a somewhat dumpy man who recently took up the distressing game. He attached himself to the "rope" pro and felt he had the feel of the swing after considerable practice with the weighted clothesline. Once he took the club in his hand, however, the feeling of familiarity inevitably disappeared.

The first time he went out to play he tried the club, but couldn't conclude a working agreement with the ball. He bemoaned his trying experience at the office.

"I understand the principle of the swing when I use the weighted rope," he said.

"In that case," said Paul Sann, the executive editor, "why use the club? Why not go out on the course and swing the rope?"

"I'm afraid of hanging myself," Sherwin said sourly.

Like Sherwin, most golfers become as dependent upon their pros as the alcoholic on his shot. Let them suffer through the mischance of two poor rounds in succession and they come running to poppa-pro to get straightened out. What they're looking for is a kind of "fix." Pros even run to other pros or read each other's books and this makes for a vicious cycle.

One pro tells you about weight transference, another stresses the necessity for pronation, and a third lectures you on the trouble you can encounter by not convoluting on the fratistration in the frenistant with your deltoids. If Al Kelly, the double-talk expert, said some of the things pros attempt to impart to the players at $4.50 a half hour, it would be no more intelligible, but far more laughable. You wouldn't play any better, but you don't in any event.

For instance, a pro once told me I was a mere sixteenth of an inch away from being a respectable golfer, but when that minute distance is translated into strokes it turns out to be the difference between pars and bogeys.

I'm not suggesting here that you deprive the pro of his chance and try to teach yourself, any more than I would suggest a spot of do-it-yourself brain surgery. But once you discover the limitations of your game—it'll take you quite a while and an abacus to count them—then, if you're wise, you will learn to enjoy the companionship of the course and stop counting the strokes when they get too astronomical.

Danny Lawler, the pro at Rock Ridge Country Club in Newtown, Connecticut, tells me that my trouble is that I lack confidence. I also lack concentration, energy, muscle control, self-composure, self-control and talent. I am past the stage where I feel I'll be able to beat the game at some foreseeable future.

"Your trouble," Lawler told me, "is that you have no faith in yourself when you get a wood in your hand. You're too anxious to hit the ball. You try to remember everything you've ever been taught while you're doing it, and you grip the club as though you're trying to mash it in your fingers. Also you get mad at yourself too easily."

"Is that all?" I asked. "That wouldn't seem enough to make me as consistently bad as I've been."

"That sarcasm," Danny said, "is another obstacle. It distracts you trying to be funny all the time. What I want from you now is an explanation of what you think your biggest problem is."

"The ball," I said.

"But it just sits there waiting to be hit," he replied.

"Yes, but it's important where 'there' is. For you it's the middle of the fairway. For me it's deep in a clump of poison ivy."

Doug Ford, the biggest money winner of that year on the pro circuit, once advised me: "Why worry about it? There isn't a golfer alive, good or bad, who has absolutely the same swing in a game as he has on the practice tee. But in your case, I believe the solution to your game is writing about it rather than playing it."

Why worry about it indeed? The trouble with most of the folks on my side of the handicap chart is that we're inclined to forget that golf is a game. We don't make a living at it, but we treat it with the grim application which must have been lavished by the Knights of the Round Table setting out in search of the Holy Grail. Actually it is absurd. Can there be anything more ludicrous than grown men and women traversing 5 or 6 miles up hill, down dale and through flora and fauna just to get a drink? A straight line across the dressing room from the locker to the bar would get us to our inevitable destination in much less roundabout fashion and we'd have approximately four more guzzling hours.

And yet people go out of their way even to interest *children* in the game, a mistake I made last spring. The circus was coming to Madison Square Garden and I'd purchased tickets long in advance to take my daughter. One thing led to another, however, and by the time our circus day came around I was involved in a golf date. Jane was furious, but I placated her by taking her to the club and allowing her to walk around the course with me.

142

From a pre-teen sullenness at having been cheated out of her show, Jane's face altered first into a snicker, then a smile, finally a loud laugh as she watched me flub my shots.

"What's tickling you?" I snarled.

"Daddy," she said, "you're funnier than the clowns."

I decided to be big about it. The child obviously has a neat sense of humor, even if her father's futility is what brings it to the surface.

Countless are the wonders which transpire on the golf course when the clubs are used for a purpose other than the manufacturer intended. Take, for example, the case of W. E. Jackson, who brought home the bacon one Sunday morning after a round on a Jacksonville, Florida, course. It seems a 200-pound wild boar rushed out of the nearby woods and charged Jackson and a companion. I would not know how accurate Mr. Jackson is when chipping toward the eighth green but against the boar he defended himself ably with a 5-iron, killed the beast, and bore home its carcass. The Jackson family was well fed for the rest of the summer on pork chops, spare ribs, ham and bacon and by early September the little Jacksons were growing tusks.

Or contemplate the experience of one Cliff Kellstrom, who played a Detroit course and scored two birdies on one shot. His second shot was wild, seemingly heading for out of bounds, but up above a mallard flew by. The errant ball struck the winging bird and rebounded toward the green. The mallard fell dead on the fairway. Kellstrom, first the golfer, holed out in four for a birdie, then returned to pick up the bird.

I've been given the bird often enough, but rarely on the wing, and seldom have I come away from the golf course well stocked with food for the stomach. Usually it's just food for thought.

If we just didn't dream of happier days ahead! The dreams are what make us come back for additional doses of punishment. In them there is a bit of the *Tragical History*

143

of Dr. Faustus, some of *Damn Yankees,* and all of Joe Hardy. We're Hogan and Snead and Souchak all wrapped in one perfect golfer. We walk up to the ball with insouciance, carelessly light a cigarette, and then with the smoke curling about our sneering lips, we lash at the ball and watch it fly.

It splits the fairway a mile away and comes to rest an iron shot from the green. The caddy has lagged a little behind. Patiently we wait, but then with just the proper tone of mild annoyance in our voice we say, "Come on, boy, how about that 8-iron? There's a par waiting."

"Sorry, sir," the boy says. "You're hitting so long today I just can't keep up."

He reaches for the 8-iron, but his hand hesitates on the club. "Seven, I think, sir. There's a wind up there."

"Not today, son," you say. "The eight's my club on this shot."

He hands you the eight. You give him a confident wink. You see him muttering a prayer. You know he's bet his day's fees on you against the club champ. You bite into that ball and it takes off from the turf, the divot jumping up to follow, but you don't see it. Your head's down. Your arms are extended in the follow-through. Your body's arched, just the way the pros tell the duffers when they're taking lessons: "Finish up high. Finish proud, like you're peeing over the fence." The ball hits the green and the backspin takes. It's a sure par, likely a bird. Oh, well, the game's so easy, sometimes it gets boring.

You feel something boring in your back. You open your eyes one at a time. Rapidly the lovely dream fades. It's the missus' elbow.

"Have you quit golf again this week-end or are you going to get up and keep your lousy date?" she asks, knowing the answer all too well. I do, too. I'm a lost soul. I'm one of the legion of the damned. I'm helplessly, hopelessly, haplessly hooked, like a herring on a line. I am pulled this way and that. I am a slave to yesterday's fancies, today's fads and the pros' advice tomorrow. I wheedle and I whine and I curse my fate, but I'm back week-end after week-end wallowing in my own discomfiture attempting to make my body do what patently it has no intention of doing. My bedside is piled high with golfing literature, which has added to my confusion and ineptitude. I may not be the best golfer, but I'm the best read.

Once I read an article which contended that the address was similar to the way a T quarterback in football stands over the center just before the snapback. It was written by the pro at West Point and used Gus Vann, Army's quarterback at the time, and Col. Red Blaik, then the Cadets' football coach, as models. The article stated that Blaik had lowered his score considerably by addressing the ball much in the manner his quarterbacks crouched behind the scrimmage line.

I adopted the theory and set out to prove its undoubted excellence. The position was uncomfortable, but I persisted until somebody asked what charade I was acting out. I explained.

"You'd better look over the defense," my querulous partner answered, "before you start calling signals."

Another time I read that a forward press was employed by the pros because it helps them to get loose before swinging. I introduced my forward press while playing with Jimmy Basile.

"What is that supposed to be that you're doing?" asked Basile.

"It's my forward press," I said. "Don't all pros forward-press?"

"You're not a pro and that isn't a forward press," said Basile. "To me it looks more like the samba."

"The samba's a dance," I said.

"And you," said Basile, "look as though you have ants in your stance."

That's not surprising. I also have butterflies in my stomach, bats in my belfry and memories in which you could chill a bottle of beer. But I just don't have the character to chuck it all and take up something safe, like bull fighting.

I have broken my heart and my resolutions, blistered my hands, tanned my body, expended endless hours, money, emotion and energy in the vain pursuit of something called par. Yet I haven't caught so much as a fleeting glimpse of it.

When Sam Snead shot his incredible 59 at Greenbrier in White Sulphur Springs I was as disgusted as a duffer could possibly be. There was something indecent about such a perfect performance, but I read every newspaper account I could find. I telephoned several golf writers I knew to ferret out any further information they may not have included in their stories of the historic event.

As I dwelt on the obscene disparity between Snead and myself, I recalled a time I played behind Sammy on the Baltusrol course a week before the Open there in 1954. The roughs fascinated me, but devoured me and my balls. They were much like woven mats of grass through which a club could not pass. Someone asked Snead later, "How do you get out of that stuff?"

"Man, you just don't get in it," Sammy drawled.

Now, that's a fine answer. It's about as helpful as telling a man about to be electrocuted, "You ought to get a charge out of that chair."

There are approximately 5,718 golf courses in play in the United States. The National Golf Foundation reports that in 1958 alone 182 new courses were built on which 2,879,000 rounds of play were charted in the first year of their operation. Another 293 courses are under construction, and 959 courses are in a planning stage. What pleasure do I derive from these statistics? I have company, that's all, and I'm going to have more.

Recently I was visiting my daughter at her summer

146

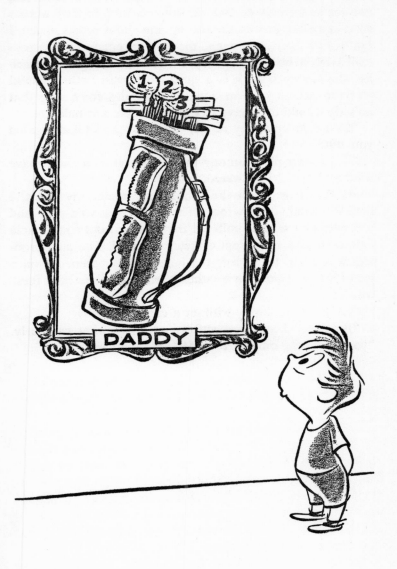

DADDY

camp, where they have a pitch-and-putt course as well as a driving range for the kids. Watching some of the children, not yet in their teens, handle irons as though they were a third appendage was depressing me dangerously when I ran across Jack Campana, the golfing coach at Erasmus Hall High School in Brooklyn, who also was golf counsellor at the camp. Jack is a quiet little man with a quaint Harvard accent and an equally charming conviction that nobody should ever have trouble hitting a golf ball.

"Come on up to my range," he said, "and I'll straighten you out."

"Take your place among the other volunteers who have tried and died," I answered.

At the range, with the rubber mat under my shoes, I couldn't do anything wrong. There were just Campana and I. I whacked several balls all the way across Pennsylvania Route 90 into an ancient cemetery beyond. The only problem was I had to retrieve the balls. One of them lay on a grave above which the weather-worn tombstone bore these words:

"He lies here happy without a care."

"Brother," I said respectfully and somewhat enviously, "you found the only sure way to beat the game."

Milton Gross is the nationally syndicated sports columnist of the *New York Post.* His perceptiveness, his delightful wit, and his ability to describe the human situation have brought him wide acclaim. He has covered as a reporter and a columnist the great sports events of the past twenty-five years, and he is an intimate of the top sports figures. He contributes frequently to magazines such as *The Saturday Evening Post* and *Sports Illustrated,* and in 1957 he won the award for the best sports story of the year.

Mr. Gross is a graduate of Fordham University, and holds a Master of Arts degree from Columbia University.